Gail,
Best wishes ∞
literacy leader
Cathy Toll

Educational
Coaching

· · · · · ·

Educational Coaching

A PARTNERSHIP
FOR PROBLEM SOLVING

Cathy A. Toll

ASCD

Alexandria, Virginia USA

1703 N. Beauregard St. • Alexandria, VA 22311-1714 USA
Phone: 800-933-2723 or 703-578-9600 • Fax: 703-575-5400
Website: www.ascd.org • E-mail: member@ascd.org
Author guidelines: www.ascd.org/write

Deborah S. Delisle, *Executive Director;* Stefani Roth, *Publisher;* Genny Ostertag, *Director, Content Acquisitions;* Carol Collins, *Senior Acquisitions Editor;* Julie Houtz, *Director, Book Editing & Production;* Liz Wegner, *Editor;* Georgia Park, *Senior Graphic Designer;* Mike Kalyan, *Director, Production Services;* Circle Graphics, *Typesetter*

All web links in this book are correct as of the publication date below but may have become inactive or otherwise modified since that time. If you notice a deactivated or changed link, please e-mail books@ascd.org with the words "Link Update" in the subject line. In your message, please specify the web link, the book title, and the page number on which the link appears.

PAPERBACK ISBN: 978-1-4166-2561-2 ASCD product #118027 n3/18

PDF E-BOOK ISBN: 978-1-4166-2563-6; see Books in Print for other formats.

Quantity discounts are available: e-mail programteam@ascd.org or call 800-933-2723, ext. 5773, or 703-575-5773. For desk copies, go to www.ascd.org/deskcopy.

Library of Congress Cataloging-in-Publication Data is available for this title.

LCCN: 2017057164

27 26 25 24 23 22 21 20 19 18   1 2 3 4 5 6 7 8 9 10 11 12

Educational
Coaching

· · · · · · ·

A PARTNERSHIP FOR PROBLEM SOLVING

Introduction

I believe that educational coaching is one of the best ways to support teacher learning and increase teacher effectiveness. Of course, I didn't always know this, and I sort of backed into my belief in coaching. In other words, I didn't set out to be a coach or to establish coaching as my top choice for supporting teachers. Rather, I tried everything else first.

Many years ago when I was a new teacher leader, I assumed I knew best what teachers needed; I thought that by being nice but assertive, I could get teachers to change in the ways I thought best. Needless to say, this approach was unsuccessful. At about the same time, I became skilled in leading workshops and did a great many presentations for teachers, trusting that those in the audience would adopt my ideas and practices. A few teachers did, but often in their own ways, which wasn't necessarily what I had hoped for. Many enjoyed the workshop but then forgot all about it. I next investigated teacher book groups and facilitated several. This was enriching for me and did lead some of my colleagues to try new things, but it didn't lead to any sustained changes in their practice.

When I became a school principal, I was most effective in supporting teachers' learning and growth when I had a strong, positive relationship with teachers and when, together, we talked about their present understanding and skills, as well as what they wished to accomplish in their classrooms. When we were mutual problem solvers, we found the partnership worthwhile. That's when I began to focus on developing my coaching skills. I started meeting my own goal of supporting teachers' transformative practices and realized that my

1

increased effectiveness resulted from starting where the teachers were, listening carefully, and collaboratively planning with them for further learning.

In the many years since, I have not only refined my skills but also learned how to coach others in developing their own skills as coaches. At the same time, I looked to research to explain both my successes and struggles, and I conducted my own research on teacher professional learning and effective coaching. I became increasingly reflective about what successful coaches—myself or others—did and didn't do, whether working in the field of preK–12 education, health care, social services, or business, and I combined my insights with knowledge about adult learning, organizational change, and leadership.

Initially, my work focused on the content area of literacy, and I worked primarily with literacy coaches. After my first book on literacy coaching was published, I started hearing from math coaches that they had borrowed copies of the book from their literacy colleagues and found it helpful. I stretched my work to include math coaches and then coaches with such titles as instructional coach, curriculum coach, content coach, and information technology (IT) coach. Soon I was consulting with coaches and coach leaders throughout the United States, as well as in Australia and Canada, and finding that I could help them all, regardless of the content area in which they worked.

A Word About This Book

This is my sixth book for coaches and my seventh addressing collaboration for professional learning. It's my first book written explicitly for coaches of all stripes—math coaches, literacy coaches, instructional coaches, or coaches with any other title—and for those who lead coaches. I have chosen *educational coach* as the umbrella term for the many kinds of coaches who work in preK–12 education.

But, you may be wondering, can one book really speak to such a wide variety of educational coaches? I find that effective coaching is the same across the many titles and tasks of coaches in schools today; good coaching is good coaching. There are differences among coaches in the content of the work they do—for instance, some coaches focus on math or English language learners—as well as in the grade range of the teachers with whom they work. That's why this book will provide examples from a range of content areas and grade levels. There are also differences in the effectiveness of the various coaching models, which I will discuss in Chapter 2. But whatever the coaches' titles or roles, this book will help them all.

I assume that you, the reader of this book, are either an educational coach or someone who supports educational coaches as an administrator, a program coordinator, or a university faculty member. You may be new to your role or may have many years' experience. I assume that, in all cases, you're interested in furthering your understanding of coaching and honing your skills as a coach or a supporter of coaches.

Three Recurring Concepts

Three concepts will recur throughout the book. They are key to my understanding of successful coaching:

- *Partnership*: Coaches and teachers are partners in the process. They collaborate as equals, with each bringing experiences and strengths to the work.

- *The problem-solving model*: After years of research, reflection, and practice, I have concluded that the problem-solving model of coaching is most effective. It promotes teacher reflection, enhances decision making, and leads to more lasting change than many other models of coaching. It also supports all kinds of teachers.

- *CAT qualities*: I can teach many skills and processes to coaches, but the coaches themselves must develop the qualities of Connectivity, Acceptance, and Trustworthiness as underpinnings for success. Without the CAT qualities, coaches will be unsuccessful. (And, no, these qualities are not particularly feline, although their initials spell the word *cat*.)

The Structure of the Book

Each of the chapters in this book begins with key questions that the chapter will address. The questions should generate reflection and expectation, but they should also resonate with readers and propel them to read on.

Each chapter then features a vignette describing a coaching situation. The examples are amalgamations of coaching situations I'm familiar with, and the coaches I describe are composites of, or have the qualities of, several coaches I have known. Thus, the vignettes reflect real life. At the end of each chapter, I revisit the vignette and explain how a coach might use information from the chapter to resolve the issue at hand. The resolutions always include two components: reflection and collaboration. These important components of teaching and leading are just as essential to problem solving in coaching.

A word about pronouns. In most cases, I use plural nouns so that I can use plural pronouns and thereby avoid gender-specific pronouns. In cases where I use examples of individual people, I alternate between the pronouns *he* and *she*. I recognize that there are people who do not use those pronouns to identify themselves and would rather use different pronouns, such as *they* or *ze*, or none at all. With apologies to such readers, I have chosen to use occasional gender-specific pronouns for ease in reading.

The chapters in this book are divided into three sections. The first section (Chapters 1 and 2) deals with coaching basics; it provides information about coaching in general, the effects of coaching, and various coaching models. The second section (Chapters 3–8) addresses coaching practices. It provides practical strategies and perspectives, beginning with the problem-solving cycle and coaching conversations and then moving on to strategies for developing relationships, communicating effectively, and working with teams. The third section (Chapters 9 and 10) addresses obstacles to coaching success, as well as tasks that coaches may be asked to engage in beyond the coaching conversation; the last chapter, Chapter 10, provides a big-picture summary of important points.

Because I want this book to feel like a conversation I'm having with readers, I only provide citations for material I refer to explicitly. Cited material appears in the reference section of the book. I also provide a narrative bibliography, where readers can find additional resources and explanations that underpin the material provided in the chapters.

My Wishes for You, the Reader

I hope this book feels like a conversation. I hope it helps you to both understand coaching and enhance your practices. I hope it leads to greater confidence in coaching among teachers, administrators, and, of course, coaches, as you grow in your recognition of educational coaching as a way to solve problems and enhance success. And I hope you will keep in touch to let me know what you've learned and how I can help. Feel free to send me a note through my website, www.partneringtolearn.com.

1

Coaching 101

> How is educational coaching defined?

> How does educational coaching differ from other forms of teacher professional development?

> What qualities do coaches need to have?

Chapter 1 Vignette

Ginger Laidlaw is a middle school curriculum coordinator who has been asked to include coaching in her work this year. She's taken the lead in furthering a schoolwide initiative to include writing in all aspects of the curriculum, so she decides to make that initiative the focus of her coaching. She announces to teachers at the back-to-school faculty meeting that she'd like to meet with teachers individually to review lesson plans and coach them to include writing in their instruction.

As Ginger meets with teachers, she finds that although they all present lesson plans that include writing, the writing is either assigned with no support or is superficial, such as writing a caption for a photo. In these meetings, she explains how to improve the lesson plans; the teachers thank her, and they part company. In follow-up coaching sessions, Ginger finds that teachers either didn't implement her suggestions or implemented them and didn't like the results. Ginger doesn't feel that her work as a coach is having any positive effect.

When coaching became popular in U.S. schools in the early 2000s, it spread quickly and according to the understanding of a variety of practitioners. As a result, there are many versions of educational coaching to be found. This chapter will provide basics about coaching that will establish a common ground from which to proceed. Whether you're highly experienced or new to coaching, I urge you to read this chapter. It's crucial for understanding the key concepts on which this book is built.

Coaching Defined

Despite the many articles and books written on educational coaching, specific definitions of coaching are hard to come by. Most agree that coaches provide a kind of professional development and that this professional development occurs in relationship to individuals and teams of teachers. From there, though, definitions are often vague or nonexistent. So for starters, let's agree on what an educational coach is.

Early in my work with coaches, I defined an educational coach as someone who helped teachers identify their strengths, grow those strengths, and develop new strengths (Toll, 2005). I developed this definition to emphasize that coaching was a positive experience for every educator, not something solely for ineffective teachers—and I stand by it. However, it is a bit general and, therefore, I've developed a second definition to accompany the first:

Educational coaches partner with teachers for job-embedded professional learning that enhances teachers' understanding of students, the curriculum, and pedagogy for the purpose of solving problems that impede teacher success and pursuing interests that enhance teacher success.

This definition has several significant components:

- Coaching is a *partnership*. It's a collaboration between equals. The coach may steer the process, but the teacher has the final say in what is discussed and what actions are taken as a result.

- Coaching is *job-embedded*, meaning that it attends to teachers' own classrooms and their own strengths, needs, and interests.

- Coaching is about *professional learning*. When coaching is effective, teachers learn.

- Coaching *enhances* teachers' capacity; coaches don't "fix" teachers or tell them what to do.

- Coaching supports reflection about *students, the curriculum, and pedagogy*. Too often, coaching processes emphasize only one aspect of the work of teaching—for instance, when coaches and teachers address only best practices or student data. Coaching partnerships must consider all three aspects of the work.

- Coaching helps teachers *enhance their success* as teachers. Teachers learn to solve problems that get in the way of their success. They also pursue interests that can increase their success, such as integrating the curriculum, developing new instructional plans, or using digital technologies.

My more precise definition of coaching is applicable to coaches with a variety of labels. It applies to math coaches, literacy coaches, instructional coaches, curriculum coaches, and others in coaching roles. Sometimes people think that a different label for the coach leads to a different definition of coaching, but I find that coaching is coaching. What changes is the focus of the coach's content or the outcome in relation to a program or subject discipline. What *doesn't* change is the purpose for coaching and the manner in which coaches and teachers collaborate.

Coaching and Other Forms of Professional Development

The criticism of "sit-and-get" approaches to professional development is well known, and educational coaching has grown in part because it provides an alternative. Interestingly, coaching can enhance even traditional approaches to professional development that consist of an expert's presentation by providing additional follow-up reflection and problem solving (Showers & Joyce, 2002). Nevertheless, many school districts are moving toward approaches to professional development that are more engaging and collaborative than presentation-style efforts, including professional learning communities or teams, book study groups, and mentoring, as well as educational coaching. In addition, schools often hire content-area specialists, such as math specialists and reading specialists, with professional development among their duties.

I'm often asked to explain the differences among the various approaches to teacher learning as they pertain to coaching. Here's a view of coaching in the contexts of professional learning communities, mentoring, study groups, and content specialization.

Coaching and Professional Learning Communities

In many schools, teachers now collaborate in small teams that typically consist of individuals from the same grade level or department. Sometimes these teams are referred to as *professional learning communities*, and sometimes they're called *professional learning teams*. I'll use the former term here for convenience.

Professional learning communities meet for a variety of purposes, sometimes explicitly laid out by school leaders and sometimes assumed by the participants. Thus, teams meet to pass on information from administrators, to develop curriculum, to analyze student data, to collaborate in planning lessons, and for many other purposes.

When professional learning communities attend to the "L" in their title—learning—there can be a role for an educational coach. Coaches, with their skill in facilitating teacher reflection and problem solving, are ideal facilitators of learning done by teams. Please note that everything in this book applies to coaches' work with teams of teachers as well as with individuals. There are some characteristics of professional learning communities that make coaching a bit more challenging, which I will address in Chapter 7.

Coaching and Mentoring

Coaching and mentoring are sometimes confused. Sometimes they overlap, but there are important differences between them. A key distinction is the difference in clients. Coaches' clients are teachers: Coaching is job-embedded and focuses on teachers' challenges and interests. In contrast, mentors have several clients. Mentors work with new teachers to help them adjust to the teaching profession, learn about district and school policies and practices, and develop their teaching practice so their students learn. Mentors' clients include administrators, teachers, and even teaching in general, given that mentoring has been promoted as a way to retain new teachers in the profession. Mentors sometimes attend to the challenges and interests of the new teachers they work with, but mentors also attend to the curriculum, human resources information, or administrative tasks. Thus, coaching is likely one of the tactics in mentors' toolkits, but, understandably, mentors must perform many other tasks as well.

Coaching and Study Groups

Another kind of small-group professional development is the study group, often organized around a topic for inquiry or a professional book. The discussion in study groups may enhance teacher knowledge and skill without any assistance from an educational coach. However, group discussions usually benefit from a facilitator, and coaches typically have skills that make them effective facilitators. Coaches' support of inquiry groups or book study groups is not educational coaching per se, but coaches' good questioning and careful listening are likely to assist such groups in furthering participants' professional learning. Tips for a coach's role in relation to study groups are found in Chapter 9.

Coaching and Content Specialization

Math and reading specialists, and occasionally other content-area specialists, have in recent years found coaching on their list of duties. Frequently, they're challenged to balance their time between coaching and other responsibilities. However, in the absence of a job description that clearly delineates the specialist's duties or of an agreement as to what percentage of time is to be devoted to coaching, the coaching role often loses out.

An additional challenge for many specialists is that they may be asked to represent their school or district administration in passing on policy information, leading curriculum implementation, or completing other tasks that put them "in charge." When these specialists shift to a coaching role, the teachers they work with may struggle to be open and vulnerable because the specialists seem more like administrators. When asked to represent the school or district

in a given task, the specialists may wish to speak in the third person, in order to clarify for teachers that they are *not* acting in a policymaker role—for instance, by saying, "The principal has asked me to share her policy on . . ." And, of course, savvy specialists will use their best coaching qualities when asked to do non-coaching duties so that the difference between their behavior when coaching and when performing other tasks is not too great.

Qualities of Effective Educational Coaches

I've given you my definition of coaching and clarified how coaching pertains to a variety of professional development contexts. But what about the coaches themselves?

Coaches begin successful partnerships when they demonstrate the following qualities:

- Connectivity: Coaches engage with their partners.

- Acceptance: Coaches welcome whatever teachers have to say and whatever efforts teachers put forth.

- Trustworthiness: Coaches respect what teachers tell them and maintain confidentiality.

Notice that Connection, Acceptance, and being Trustworthy create the acronym CAT. If you want to be clever, you can use cat imagery and cat-related phrases to help remember the three qualities. For instance, you and your coach colleagues might wear cat-shaped pins to remind yourselves of your coach qualities of connectivity, acceptance, and being trustworthy. Or you might think of being a *cool cat* or *the cat's meow* when you engage effectively as a coach. (C.A.T., by the way, are also my initials—coincidence, I assure you.)

Some coaches seem naturally inclined to connect, accept, and be trustworthy, whereas others have to work at it, but every coach can develop the CAT qualities described below.

Connectivity

To connect with teachers, coaches must be attentive and mentally present. Coaches who worry about an interaction they previously had with their teacher partners or who are thinking ahead to the next meeting of the day are not likely to connect with the teachers with whom they're presently working.

To strengthen their ability to connect well, coaches might develop practices to enhance their attentiveness. Some coaches practice meditation or yoga. Some use prayer, music, or nature to enhance their focus on the moment. Others use visual reminders, such as a sticky note on the corner of their tablet on which they've written "now." Sitting quietly and taking some deep breaths before a coaching conversation can be helpful as well.

Coaches must reach out to the teachers with whom they wish to connect. In other words, coaches shouldn't wait for teachers to approach them. (As a teacher, you wouldn't sit at your desk and wait for students to ask you to teach them, would you?) I encourage coaches to start the school year by scheduling a meeting with each teacher with whom they wish to connect, with the goal of engaging teachers in the problem-solving cycle through coaching conversations.

Occasionally when coaches approach teachers to arrange a meeting, the teachers beg off, saying they're too busy. Similarly, when coaches and teachers have arranged to meet, teachers will occasionally fail to show up at the scheduled time. In both situations, coaches are wise to persist in a gentle way. If teachers say they're busy, patiently ask when they will indeed have time. If teachers fail to show up, find them later that day or the next morning and get another meeting on the calendar. Continue to reach out until a meeting does occur.

Acceptance

Successful educational coaches are accepting of all teacher partners, despite any differences that exist. The biggest obstacles to acceptance are coaches' judgment and fear. Judgment gets in the way when coaches listen to their partners with an ear for catching something that is wrong, either because it doesn't accurately represent the coach's understanding or because it seems like a bad idea. Coaches who want to be more receptive to their partners might practice saying to themselves, "and this" in response to what they hear, as shorthand for, "and this is part of the conversation that I accept as well." Thus, when a teacher says, "I don't think my students like to read!" a coach might mentally think, "and this" and continue listening, without becoming distracted by whether she agrees or disagrees with the teacher's statement. It's mind training for responding in a neutral manner.

Acceptance can also be blocked by fear, usually because coaches worry that their partnership with a teacher will lead to something that makes them look bad. For instance, when a teacher tells a coach that she wants her students to memorize the Preamble to the U.S. Constitution and the coach knows that the class includes students with individualized education programs (IEPs) who will never be able to memorize that text, the coach may feel a need to quickly quash the teacher's idea. To remain accepting, coaches might shore up their attentiveness skills and then ask good questions about what their teacher partners have in mind. When coaches learn more, they show their receptiveness and sometimes quell their fears because they may learn that their teacher partners have a more reasoned plan than they thought. In addition, when coaches steer teachers through the problem-solving cycle, they help their teacher partners enhance their decision-making processes to better decide for themselves what instructional practices will be best.

Trustworthiness

Trustworthiness is tricky because coaches cannot really practice their trustworthiness until they have something to be trustworthy about. In other words, teachers have to do something or tell something to the coach before coaches can show they can be trusted with that information or observation—and often teachers need to trust coaches to engage in doing or telling something from the start.

To optimize the chances that this dance of trustworthiness can begin, coaches should meet with teacher partners in a private space with the door closed. They can also tell the teacher in advance that coaching is like Las Vegas—what happens there, stays there—and they can talk about what they do or don't share from their meetings and notes. Beyond that, however, coaches establish trustworthiness most when they honor the confidentiality of the coaching partnership as it unfolds.

Coaches should never share information with principals, department chairs, or others when it could influence the supervisory process. This is true even when the information is positive. For instance, if a curriculum coach reports to the school principal that a teacher is doing a great job of implementing the new science program, and the principal then compliments the teacher on what the coach told her, that teacher may worry about what else the principal and coach may be sharing—and others who overhear may worry if they were *not* complimented. (More on the principal–coach relationship in Chapter 8.)

Successful teaching experience is another prerequisite for building trust in the coaching partnership. Coaches' experiences as teachers provide essential knowledge to undergird their conversations with teachers, and it builds trust among teacher partners who feel reassured that the coach is "one of us." However, educational coaches don't need to be experts in all aspects of teaching. For instance, coaches with a background in teaching social studies may very well be effective in working with teachers from all content disciplines, and coaches who have taught only in the primary grades are often effective coaches for teachers in all grades of an elementary school. After all, coaches and teachers are partners, and each brings knowledge and insights to the work. Coaches don't have to know it all.

In fact, coaches who try to "know it all" are usually unsuccessful. Coaching is not telling! When educational coaches approach their work as the expert in content knowledge or teaching skill, they typically end up doing all the work in the partnership. At best, this leads teachers to over-rely on coaches' expertise; at worst, it leads to resentment on the part of teachers who feel underappreciated and without a say in the process.

The most effective educational coaches are those who connect with their teacher partners by listening carefully and asking questions that draw out teachers' knowledge, as well as their beliefs and perspectives. Educational coaches should be viewed as experts *for their process expertise*. In other words, the most effective educational coaches are skilled in helping others reflect, solve problems, and collaborate and who then accept what they learn and hold it in trust.

Educational Coaching—It's Not Athletic Coaching

The term *coach* often causes educators to think of athletic coaches. Here in Wisconsin, where I live, the Green Bay Packers football team is beloved, and the memory of the Packers' most famous coach, Vince Lombardi, looms large. Lombardi exemplified the direct, no-nonsense, hard-driving approach to athletic coaching that the term *coaching* often conjures up. But is the athletic coach a model for educational coaches?

It's valuable to think of differences among athletic coaches who coach in highly competitive settings, such as the National Football League in the United States, and athletic coaches who work in less competitive settings, say, middle schools. When the goal is to win, coaches are often no-nonsense and tough, whereas coaching for more developmental purposes, to help the individual grow, is typically more supportive and softer. Because the purpose of educational coaching is to promote teachers' growth, educational coaches are more effective using a supportive approach. We're not trying to win the Super Bowl of teaching!

Conclusion

Although there are a variety of approaches to teacher professional development, educational coaching is distinctive in that it creates partnerships that help teachers enhance their success by solving problems and pursuing topics of interest. Coaches are most successful when they have the qualities of connectivity, acceptance, and trustworthiness.

Chapter 1 Vignette Revisited

Ginger Laidlaw initially felt ineffective as a coach. To turn things around, she realized that she needed a clearer sense of exactly what she was expected to do as a coach and how she might perform those coaching duties most effectively. To accomplish these goals, she visited with and shadowed two educational coaches in her school district, read several books on coaching, and engaged in discussions with her principal, with whom she developed a job description.

After a great deal of reflection, Ginger reshaped her work with teachers. Her goal is still to support the writing initiative in the school, but rather than checking teachers' lesson plans and telling them how to improve, she engages teachers in problem-solving coaching conversations that address teachers' interests and challenges in relation to writing.

She begins each conversation with the question, "When you think about including writing in your courses, what seems to get in the way?" This initial question opens the door for teachers to talk about the obstacles they face, which range from pressure to teach other aspects of the curriculum to teachers' lack of knowledge about how to help students improve their writing. Ginger and the teachers have developed plans to solve such problems and to use data to gauge success. In these ways, Ginger is able to effectively support teachers as they implement the writing initiative.

2

Coaching for Change

> What difference do coaches make?

> How does educational coaching lead to change?

> Does change always have to be difficult?

Chapter 2 Vignette

Jorge Flores is a math coach at Lincoln Elementary School. As he reflects on his first two years in the position, he feels frustrated. He looks back on his logs and sees that he has interacted with every teacher in the school in some manner. He also notices that he's arriving at school at 7 a.m. and often staying until after 5 p.m.; he's putting in a lot of effort! On any given day, Jorge is in classrooms doing demonstration lessons and helping teachers use the math materials that were purchased for the new curriculum. After school, he often meets with grade-level teams to help them plan lessons. On half-days allocated for schoolwide professional development, Jorge leads workshops on best practices in math instruction. When there's a meeting of an intervention team, Jorge attends and suggests teaching materials and practices that teachers can use to help students who are not experiencing success. And yet when he looks at teachers' practices and evidence of student learning, he doesn't see any effect of his coaching. Jorge decides that he needs to find a better approach to coaching over the summer months and then will give it one more year. If at the end of his third year as a coach he still doesn't feel effective, he will return to his own classroom.

Educational coaches are in the change business. Their jobs wouldn't exist if someone didn't want something to change. Often, positions for coaches are created because a school administrator wants a coach to help teachers become more effective in implementing a program, raising test scores, or complying with new policies. Sometimes educational coaching is offered as a path to something more general, such as improved professional development or teacher effectiveness. In any event, with coaching comes the sense that something should change.

The goal of this chapter is to help educational coaches and administrators think about change. The ideas presented here can truly transform how coaches conceptualize their work.

Changes Produced by Educational Coaching

The body of research on coaching has grown significantly over the last 15 years. Some studies point to coaching's effect on student achievement, although such evidence is difficult to produce because coaches' clients are teachers, not students; when student achievement improves, it may very well be due to coaching, but it might also be due to a condition that led to both effective coaching and greater student achievement. For instance, research shows that certain kinds of principal leadership, such as engaged leadership that focuses on learning and flexible implementation of initiatives, support both successful coaching and increased student achievement. It's difficult to parse out the effects of various phenomena to say exactly what might lead to student achievement.

However, we know that there are characteristics of effective teachers that lead to greater student achievement, and we have evidence that educational coaching can enhance those characteristics. For instance, educational coaching can lead to greater teacher reflection, and teacher reflection can lead to greater student achievement. Other effects of educational coaching include increased collaboration, better use of data, and more effective decision making. Such enhancements are desirable in all schools and likely will lead to greater student learning.

Educational coaching can make a difference, but the differences achieved are not all the same. Some approaches to coaching lead to deeper, more lasting changes, and some lead to more superficial or short-lived changes.

Four Models of Coaching and Subsequent Change

The type of change that occurs through coaching reflects, in part, the model of coaching used. After studying various approaches over many years, I've concluded that coaching models can be clustered into four categories, based on how teachers are expected to change as a result of coaching endeavors.

Models Focused on What Teachers Do

Some models of coaching focus on teachers' practices, with an emphasis on helping teachers to do something different in their classrooms. When working within these behavioral models, educational coaches typically observe teachers to identify which best practices they're implementing and which ones they might add to their repertoire. Often, coaches then demonstrate new practices in the teachers' classrooms and follow up by supporting teachers in implementing the practices themselves.

A focus on teachers' behaviors seems like a logical approach to coaching because the most visible aspect of teaching is what teachers *do*. After all, effective teachers implement instructional strategies that can be observed and described. As a result of this logic, this behavior-focused approach to coaching is popular; in fact, an emphasis on changing teachers' behaviors is a common approach to teacher professional development in general.

Surprisingly, professional development focused on what teachers do is among the least effective approaches. Think about changes you've made to your own behaviors. It can be easy to wake up one morning and decide to go for a walk or eat a healthy breakfast as a change in your before-work activity, but it may be quite difficult to maintain that changed behavior over time because behavior change is not "sticky." In other words, it's quite simple to decide to do something different, but *continuing* to do something different is often a challenge. After a day or two of eating that healthy breakfast or exercising in the early morning, many people will return to their previous hit-the-snooze-alarm-and-grab-a-donut behavior!

Similarly, when educational coaches demonstrate a new practice, their teacher partners may eagerly try the practice themselves, but in a matter of days or weeks, the teachers may give it up. Perhaps the new practice was difficult to implement, did not fit the teachers' particular class situation, failed to solve a problem that the teachers were trying to solve, or even created new problems. Adopting a new practice is challenging, and it's often easier to let it go than to make it work.

Models Focused on How Teachers Feel

Some approaches to coaching are based on the idea that educational coaches should help teachers feel excited, interested, or committed to their work in general or to an innovation in particular. These models of coaching have improved teacher affect as the desired outcome. Within these models, educational coaches focus on building teachers' trust, developing teachers' confidence, and ensuring that teachers have "bought into" whatever initiatives are being implemented in the school.

Although emotions and positive feelings play an important role in teachers' work, I'm not aware of evidence that links teachers' positive feelings to student achievement. Clearly, teachers need to trust coaches and feel good about the coaching process. However, coaching programs that primarily focus on supporting teachers' positive feelings will not necessarily lead to greater student learning.

Models Focused on Teacher Thinking

Some models of coaching enhance teachers' reflection and decision making. When working within these models, educational coaches invite teachers to reflect on the content of teaching (curriculum, standards, and benchmarks); evidence of student learning (often in the form of data); and teaching practices (pedagogy). Teachers then use what they've learned to solve problems and pursue new initiatives.

Think again about those people who decide to start the day in a healthier way. That decision is probably based on their understanding of the health benefits of exercise or certain food choices. Whether or not they succeed in acting on that knowledge over the long run, they will not forget the information. Similarly, the understanding that teachers develop in some models of coaching will last.

Research and theory support increasing teachers' attention to content, pedagogy, and data, as well as increasing teachers' reflection, as paths to improving student achievement. When coaches help teachers enhance their understanding and decision making, they help teachers deepen their thinking; unlike changes in behavior, changes in thinking are, indeed, "sticky." Coaching that focuses on enhanced teacher thinking has a lasting effect on both teachers and students.

Models Focused on Teacher Collaboration

Teachers might collaborate with one another in any model of coaching. For instance, some models of coaching aim to have teachers work in small groups to learn new practices or deepen their understanding and skill at problem solving, and there are certainly teams of teachers that meet to commiserate or encourage one another. However, some models of coaching have collaboration as an explicit outcome. Within these models, coaches focus on helping teams of teachers develop their collaborative skills.

Typically, when coaches aim to develop teacher collaboration, they do so by facilitating meetings of professional learning teams (PLTs) or professional learning communities (PLCs). The nature of this facilitation depends on which of the previous three outcomes the coaches and team members pursue. Changing practices, feelings, or thinking requires different coaching tactics.

The chart in Figure 2.1 summarizes the four models of coaching.

The Best Model?

I favor models of coaching that enhance teacher thinking, whether conducted one-to-one or in collaborative efforts with teams. These approaches lead to changes in teachers—greater reflection, more effective problem solving, more informed decision making—that benefit students.

Please note that the four areas of coaching focus refer to the desired outcome of coaching, not to the activities of particular coaches. At any given moment, an educational coach might be addressing teachers' practices, feelings, understandings, or collaborative skills; it's the *focus* of the program in which the coach works that reflects the model.

For instance, let's say that a high school curriculum coach is working within an intellectual model of coaching that focuses on teacher problem

FIGURE 2.1 **Models of Coaching**			
MODEL	**FOCUS**	**GOAL**	**COACH'S TASKS**
Behavioral	Focus is on what teachers do	Implementation of best practices	Coaches observe and give teachers feedback on their practices, then demonstrate new practices and assist teachers in implementing them.
Affective	Focus is on how teachers feel	Increased teacher satisfaction and comfort with changes	Coaches act as cheerleaders in supporting teachers, pointing out their strengths and successes, and promote initiatives by highlighting their positive qualities.
Intellectual	Focus is on what teachers think	Teacher inquiry, problem solving, and decision making	Coaches help teachers analyze student data, understand the curriculum, and reflect on pedagogy, then solve problems inhibiting success.
Collaborative	Focus is on how teachers work together	Creation of learning communities	Coaches facilitate teams in developing new practices, supporting one another, or deepening reflection and understanding.

Source: From *Lenses on Literacy Coaching: Conceptualizations, Functions, and Outcomes* (p. 46), by C. A. Toll, 2007, Norwood, MA: Christopher-Gordon.

solving. The coach spends much of her time meeting with department-level teams to facilitate their identification of problems in implementing the curriculum and to help them solve those problems. She has recently met with a team of science teachers who have been studying the crosscutting concepts identified by the Next Generation Science Standards. The outcome of this coaching work is for the science teachers to understand the crosscutting concepts and think about them in relation to their teaching.

However, during her engagements with the teachers, she finds herself initially helping them attend to the strong feelings of the two most experienced teachers that once again they are addressing a new set of standards that they have had no say in developing. As the group moves into its exploration of the crosscutting concepts identified in the standards, questions arise about instructional strategies for teaching those concepts, and the group spends a good deal of time looking at resources available to answer those questions. Thus, this coach helped teachers with their feelings about the standards and with their practical questions about bringing the standards to life in their classrooms, within a model of coaching that focused on helping the teachers think deeply about the crosscutting concepts.

Inevitably, in all their coaching work, coaches deal with practice, feelings, and thinking. However, having a clear understanding of the focus of the coaching *program* will provide direction for educational coaches and will help teachers know what to expect. It will also help to evaluate the effect of coaching. For instance, if the desired outcome is increased teacher problem solving when implementing a new instructional program, it would be ineffective to evaluate the coaches' work by gauging teachers' feelings.

The Struggle to Change

"Change is hard." "Change is always painful." "No one wants to change." These axioms are repeated in many settings when the topic of change arises—but they don't always describe reality. There certainly are difficult and painful changes, such as letting go of a dying parent or being unexpectedly transferred by an employer. On the other hand, there are pleasant and joyful changes, such as moving into a new home or welcoming a baby into the family. The key factor in determining whether a change is welcomed or resisted seems to be how much control a person has over it. In general, the more a person *chooses* to change, the more the change is palatable or even enjoyable. Peter Senge captured this idea when he quoted a consultant's words: "People don't resist change. They resist being changed!" (Senge et al., 1999, p. 332).

This concept about change is important for educational coaches. Coaching is not about changing people by telling them what to change. It's about supporting people in the changes *they* choose to make. Now, lest this sound too laissez-faire, let me assure you that a skilled coach who has mastered processes for helping teachers identify and solve problems is valuable to the change process.

Educational coaches can help teachers to be clear in understanding obstacles to success, setting goals for overcoming obstacles, planning to try something different, and ensuring that their efforts lead to greater success. But coaches and teachers need to start where teachers are—and teachers must be in the lead in determining what to change.

Sometimes teachers need to be told what to do, but that's a boss's job, usually enacted by school principals. Even in those cases, principals often work with teachers from a coaching stance rather than a top-down manager's stance because most principals, too, know that forcing change on others is a long and difficult struggle. However, when a change must be demanded of teachers, it is indeed principals (or other school district supervisors) who take on that responsibility. Conversely, coaches support teachers in their change processes; they don't demand change.

Conclusion

The changes brought about by educational coaching vary according to the model of coaching being implemented. Those models that enhance teachers' thinking—their reflection, problem solving, and decision making—will lead to strong, lasting effects in increasing teachers' success. When teachers are active participants in making changes, they likely will feel more positive about the process and results.

Chapter 2 Vignette Revisited

Jorge Flores spent the summer between his second and third years as a math coach looking for a better way to do his work. He attended a three-day workshop on educational coaching that caused him to rethink his approach. He followed up by reading some books and articles and then began developing a plan for the following school year.

Jorge realized that he had focused on helping teachers change their practices, emphasizing techniques for intervention and strategies for using the math instructional materials. He knew these were important skills, but after learning and reflecting, he realized that his coaching needed to shift to engaging teachers in deeper understanding and reflection. Jorge recognized that, up to that point, he had been doing the thinking for teachers regarding how they might address instructional dilemmas or provide greater support to students. Teachers saw themselves as passive recipients of practices they would try once and either adopt or, more often, dismiss.

Jorge began the next school year by explaining to teachers his interest in thinking with them about the curriculum, student data, and good teaching. He said that he wanted to support them in reflecting on what they knew and what they wanted to accomplish and then help them set goals and determine how they would meet those goals.

Some teachers were hesitant to engage in this new approach. They told Jorge that they would prefer that he just tell them what to do. Jorge saw this response as another indication that his previous approach to coaching was flawed because it enabled teachers to be passive recipients of his work. Over the course of the next several months, he helped his teacher partners recognize that his new coaching practices were helping them to more successfully do what they had been doing all along—that is, think about students' learning and their own work in support of learning—but this time with a coaching partner.

3

Coaching for Problem Solving

> What's an effective model my school can adopt for its coaching program?

> Is there a path that coaches can follow to make coaching processes smooth and effective?

> Where does the coaching process begin?

Chapter 3 Vignette

Shaun Williams, a new literacy coach at Roosevelt High School, is eager to help his colleagues, but he doesn't know where to start. He has had friendly conversations with several teachers, but the conversations don't lead anywhere. Shaun has shared some articles that he finds interesting, has offered to do demonstration lessons in teachers' classrooms, and has invited teachers for coffee and a chat. None of this establishes a process for Shaun's work as a coach. Shaun feels frustrated with his situation and disappointed in himself.

Coaches support their teacher partners by helping them solve problems that get in the way of their success. That work begins with the problem-solving cycle, which starts with the identification of an obstacle to success, and moves through three phases: *Understanding* that obstacle; *Deciding* upon a goal in

25

order to move past the obstacle; and *Trying* something new in order to meet the goal.

Starting with Obstacles

Early in my work as an educational coach, I experimented with several ways to start the coaching conversation. Some of the questions I asked were, "How's it going?" "What's going on in your classroom these days?" and "What are you thinking about in relation to your teaching?" Questions such as these sometimes led to a conversation, but often the responses were brief or general and provided little direction for further discussion. One day I gave this question a try: "When you think about the learning you want your students to do and the teaching you want to do, what gets in the way?" Teachers responded quickly and with details that enabled further conversation. I had found a winning question.

Although my discovery of what I now call The Question came from trial and error, I now understand why it's an effective way to start the coaching conversation. Simply put, humans are hardwired to put energy into reducing pain, whether physical, mental, or emotional. We lose weight because we're tired of huffing and puffing our way up the stairs, we clean the garage because we're sick of scraping the side of the car on the lawn mower, and we develop a budget because we don't like the feeling of worrying about what we can afford.

Similarly, too, teachers can easily identify their points of pain. Sometimes teachers choose not to share their problems with a coach whom they don't know well (something I will address in Chapter 8), but they *do* know where they struggle. A mistake some new coaches make is thinking that they, as coaches, understand teachers better than teachers understand themselves. This simply isn't the case.

I have been asked whether the problem-solving model is too negative because it begins with problems getting in the way of teachers' success. That isn't my experience. Most teachers are usually delighted by the opportunity to delve into a substantive issue and collaborate to solve a problem. It's refreshing to them to feel that the coaching conversation is practical and results-oriented. Many say that they are relieved to finally talk about an issue that has been plaguing them and to see that, together, we can make things better.

"What Gets in the Way?"

So how does a coach know what's getting in the way of a teacher's success? Ask! Use The Question: "When you think about the learning you want your students to do and the teaching you want to do, what gets in the way?" Find variations on this question in Figure 3.1.

Starting with a strong question is important because it provides the foundation for the entire conversation. Savvy coaches avoid questions that ask teachers what needs to be fixed, what they want to work on, or what the coach should do. Rather, they ask teachers to describe their work and its challenges. Typically, coaches invite their teacher partners to reply with as many responses as possible to generate many possible areas for exploration.

Here's an example of how the start to a problem-solving cycle might go:

Coach: Thanks for meeting with me, Jacqueline. Let's start with this question: When you think about the learning you want your students to do and the teaching you want to do, what gets in the way?

Teacher: The students just don't care. I try to get them excited about social studies, but they're more interested in their cell phones!

Coach: I'm making a note of that [writes on notepad]. What else gets in the way?

Teacher: Well, the textbook is boring and is difficult for some students, especially the English language learners.

FIGURE 3.1
The Question and Variations

Use any of the following questions when starting a problem-solving cycle:

- When you think about the learning you want your students to do and the teaching you want to do, what gets in the way?
- When you think about what you want students to learn about [content discipline] and how you want to teach about [content discipline], what gets in the way of success?
- When you think about implementing [a new initiative], what might get in the way of success for you and the students?
- When you think about bringing [standard] to life in your classroom, what might get in the way?

Coach: OK, I hear that, in addition to students' lack of caring, the textbook is boring and difficult for some. What else gets in the way?

Teacher: I can't get the kids to do their assignments, so I have them do all the work in class, which really cuts into the class time available for other things.

Coach: Let's see, I have on this list these items: Students don't care. The textbook is boring. The textbook is hard for some students to read. The students don't do their assignments. What else?

Teacher: Well, I don't have enough time to plan. Bob [department colleague] does some really fun things with his 9th graders, but he's been teaching for at least 20 years. I'm in my third year and still overwhelmed.

Coach: OK, I'm adding lack of time to plan to the list. What else?

Teacher: [long pause] I think that's it.

Coach: I'm going to read the list one more time. As I do, please select one item that you'd like to focus on first. The list consists of the following: Students don't care about social studies; the textbook is boring; the textbook is difficult for some students; students don't do their assignments; there's lack of time for planning.

Teacher: [pause] I think I'd like to start with the students not doing their assignments.

In this conversation, the coach helped the teacher consider many things getting in the way of success before choosing one to work on. This process enables teachers to air many of the obstacles they're facing, rather than merely jumping to the first thing that comes to mind. It ensures the conversation begins with a topic that's important to the teacher. Savvy coaches will keep the list that was developed and use it at the start of a subsequent problem-solving cycle, inviting teachers to add to the list additional items that appear significant at that point.

Sometimes teachers begin the coaching conversation themselves, stating what they would like to address in the partnership—for instance, when a teacher declares, "I know what I want you to do. I want you to help me develop some new assessments for my reading program!" Wise coaches might respond by saying something like, "I hear that you're seeking new assessments. Let's back up, though. I'd like to ask you this question: When you think about the learning you want your students to do and the teaching you wish to do, what gets in the way?" In this manner, coaches can slow teachers down, listen carefully, and develop a methodical system for the direction in which the conversation will go.

Sometimes teacher partners will identify several things getting in the way of success and then return to their original topic, but just as often they will recognize a different matter on which they want to focus. For instance, in the case of the teacher who wanted help coming up with new assessments, as she itemized what was getting in the way of success, she identified her struggle in using assessment information to understand students as readers. She (and her coach partner) recognized that she didn't need more assessments; she needed to learn how to make good use of the ones she was currently using.

Understanding

In the next phase of the problem-solving cycle, the partners seek to understand the problem or situation more deeply. Coaches facilitate this understanding by asking many questions to explore all aspects of the topic. Figure 3.2 suggests a variety of questions to ask based on the kind of problem being discussed.

The goal of this step is twofold: to understand the topic more deeply and to slow down the decision-making process. In the everyday rush of life in schools, quick decision making seems practical and sometimes necessary. However, when the challenge relates to the success of students and teachers, hurried responses are often guesses. Educators may decide to try something different based on nothing more than an idea that has popped into their head, and the result is often disappointing. Trial and error isn't good for either kids or teachers. Rather, when educators spend time understanding a problem or situation and then setting an appropriate goal, they're much more likely to use that understanding and that goal to develop a plan of action that will succeed.

I'm especially concerned about the quick-solution approach when working with teacher teams. So often, a teacher on a team will pose a problem, and others will quickly provide solutions without really understanding the problem. For instance, a teacher may say, "I have students who don't do their homework," and other teachers will reply, "Contact their parents!" "Use a homework

FIGURE 3.2

Possible Questions for the Understanding Phase of the Problem-Solving Cycle

Topic: A student's lack of success

- What do you notice about this student?
- When does the student seem to struggle?
- What does the student seem interested in?
- What does the student succeed in?
- Do you know how the student did last year? The year before?
- What assessment information do you have? (Coaches may want to break this question down by kinds of assessments, such as, "What do the student's results on the state assessment tell you? How does the student do on the [curriculum-based assessment]? What other assessments have you used?")
- How does the student do on assignments?
- What do the student's parents or guardians tell you?
- Has anyone else provided information?
- What have you tried?
- If this problem is solved, what will it look like?

Topic: A challenge provided by the curriculum

- What seems hard about this unit/chapter/topic?
- What have you noticed in your classroom when you teach it?
- Do you notice that all students struggle with it or only some? Which students?
- What information do you have about what the students learned previously that is related to the unit/chapter/topic?
- Do you have any data about student learning in this area?
- What instructional strategies have you used?
- Where do you think the problem lies: with the curriculum, the materials, the students, or the instruction?
- Do you know what other teachers do when they come to this unit/chapter/topic?
- What have you tried already to address this problem?
- If this problem were solved, what would it look like?

Topic: A challenge with the learning environment (disruptions, physical discomfort, student activity, and so on that make it difficult for students to learn)

- What is going on in the classroom when this occurs?
- Do all students struggle with this? If not, which students struggle?
- Do you have any ideas about why some students are not struggling?
- Why do you think this makes learning difficult?
- Have you noticed this all year or just recently?
- Do you know what other teachers are doing about this?
- What have you tried?
- If this problem were solved, what would it look like?

sheet." "Have buddies remind each other about homework." "No homework, no recess." These teachers want to help, and usually they're sharing what has worked for them. However, until they know more about the situation, their suggestions may or may not be pertinent. In the case of students who don't do homework, it may be that the teacher who raises the issue has already tried everything suggested, or that the students failing to do homework are babysitting younger siblings in the evening, or that some students don't know how to do the homework, or myriad other reasons. Providing quick solutions leads to many unsuccessful outcomes. Nonetheless, teachers often try to implement these quickly raised solutions, particularly when the teachers with challenges are less experienced than the ones with solutions.

Coaches sometimes wonder which questions to ask to gain better understanding of the problem. I ask any question that comes to mind that might be relevant. Again, look at the sample questions in Figure 3.2 for some suggestions.

The metaphor of someone using a metal detector on the beach is helpful here. The person looking for treasures doesn't know where something valuable might be buried under the sand, so she uses a wide sweep of her arm, trying to cover as much ground as possible with the detector. Similarly, a coach wants to ask questions that cover many aspects of the situation because he doesn't know where the valuable information might lie.

Taking time to understand a problem or situation is a case of going slow to go fast. Once more information is accessed and understood by all partners, effective next steps likely will be clearer.

Learning in Order to Understand

Sometimes, teachers don't have answers for the questions raised by their coach partners. In those instances, coaches and teachers can learn together by gathering more data; reaching out to others (such as other teachers, school district resource people, or students' parents); looking at professional literature; or turning to any other resource that will shed light on the situation at hand.

I encourage coaches to facilitate this process by noting questions that remain unanswered. For instance, if a teacher has identified a problem related to a subset of students who are English language learners, the coach might ask some questions to which the teacher doesn't know the answer, such as the English knowledge of the students' parents or differences in phonetic rules between the students' first language and English. The coach can make note of these unanswered questions and then, after all questions have been asked, she and the teacher can review the unanswered questions and decide which ones are worth pursuing.

When coaches and teachers identify areas in which they want to learn more, they might develop a chart that lists each question, possible resources for finding more information, and which of them will pursue the answer. The partners can divvy up the tasks and come back together a week or two later to share what they learned. Sometimes, coaches and teachers decide to learn together and use a scheduled coaching session to read an article or peruse a website together.

Deciding

Once the problem is understood, it's important to establish a goal. Coaches' final question in the Understanding phase of the problem-solving cycle might be, "If this problem were solved, what would it look like?" Teachers' responses to that question often lead to the establishment of a goal, as illustrated by the examples below.

Coach: If this problem were solved, what would it look like?

Teacher: Well, all of the students would understand what we mean by 1/2, 1/4, and 1/3.

Coach: Can you state that as a goal?

Teacher: 100 percent of students will pass the unit test on fractions.

* * * * * *

Coach: If this problem were solved, what would it look like?

Teacher: Things would stop breaking or disappearing in the lab!

Coach: Can you state that as a goal?

Teacher: All lab equipment will be returned intact to the proper place at the end of the class period.

* * * * * *

Coach: If this problem were solved, what would it look like?

Teacher: Students would actually use the vocabulary that I teach them.

Coach: Can you state that as a goal?

Teacher: Students use new vocabulary studied in class in their writing and in their conversations.

Sometimes a teacher is unable to describe what it would look like if the problem were solved; she hesitates or provides only a vague response. In that case, the coach should return to asking questions to help the teacher think further about the situation and then ask the teacher again at a later point. Occasionally, teachers reply to the question about what it would look like with statements such as, "Oh, I'd be so relieved!" or "It would be really pleasant in the classroom." Savvy coaches accept these feeling-based responses and then probe further with a question such as, "And what would I notice is different if I visited the classroom or chatted with you about your students' learning?" This follow-up question likely will enable the teacher to describe the outcome in a more concrete way.

When a teacher offers a possible goal, the coach may want to provide feedback to help refine the statement. For instance, the goal may be too broad, such as "All students will solve their math problems successfully," or narrow, such as "Every 1st grader will use a capital letter when writing the month of the year." Coaches can assist teachers in finding the Goldilocks goal that feels just right.

Brainstorming Ways to Reach the Goal

The next step in this phase of problem solving is to brainstorm how teachers might reach the goal. True brainstorming is the best option, with coaches and teachers contributing to a list of possible activities without stopping to judge each idea's worth. If neither coaches nor teachers have many ideas, then it's worthwhile for the partners to turn to additional resources to learn, just as they learned together in the Understanding phase. For instance, to develop a stronger list of ways to meet the goal, teachers might interview some other teachers, coaches might turn to content specialists in the discipline being considered, the partners might seek ideas from professional journals or websites, or both might meet with a specialist in a specific area of student needs, such as an educator with expertise in functional behavior analysis. It's valuable in all these instances to keep the goal in mind so as not to get distracted.

After a list of brainstormed possibilities for meeting the goal is developed, the teacher selects one to try. That decision should be entirely up to the teacher. Coaches occasionally find that their teacher partners have selected an action plan that differs from the one they would have chosen. Savvy coaches recognize that there is often more than one way to approach a problem and that they don't have all the answers. Coaches should express disagreement with a teacher's choice only if it will endanger students, will violate policy, or is guaranteed not to work.

Trying

In this last part of the problem-solving cycle, coaches help teachers plan for and implement the action they selected as a way to meet the goal. Typically, the action is broken down into steps, with an approximate timeline given. It's helpful to note what resources might be needed as well. Figure 3.3 provides an example of a chart a teacher might use to implement writing as a tool in mathematics. The coach and teacher used backward planning to develop the chart. First, the coach asked the teacher to describe the final state in implementing the plan, then the step just before finishing, then the step before that. This backward approach appeals to some people and in some situations; others prefer to go forward from a starting point and think about each step that will need to be accomplished to reach the final state. In either case, it is useful also to identify the resources— human and material—that may be useful at each step and an estimated timeline identifying when the steps will be completed.

When planning to try something new, it's important to plan how to gauge success. Too often, we educators try something new and decide whether it's valuable based on a gut-level response, such as, "That was fun!" or "That was too much work!" A more systematic process for assessing success in meeting the goal is worthwhile.

It's valuable to develop the plan for evaluation at the same time as one is planning action steps; if teachers and coaches wait until the end of the imple-mentation process, they may miss opportunities to collect information earlier. For

FIGURE 3.3
A Sample Action Plan

Goal: Students understand concepts and processes in unit on metric measurement, using writing as a tool.

STEP	RESOURCES NEEDED	TIMELINE
1. Analyze the unit on metric measurement for difficult spots.	Curriculum document, textbook, teacher's manual	January 2–8
2. Develop a writing activity for each difficult spot, requiring students to explain a concept or process to another student, a parent, or the class guinea pig.	List of difficult spots developed in previous step	January 9–15
3. Obtain fun writing papers for students to use.	Catalog from school supply store, box of extra paper, materials in supply closet	January 2–15
4. Review the characteristics of effective personal letters.		January 16–17
5. Write the first explanation as a class, to a different class.	Whiteboard, printer	January 18–19
6. Assign additional explanations as identified in Step 1, and support students in writing them.	Fun writing paper, my notebook to record student successes and needs	January 22–31

instance, a pre- and post-measure may be helpful in determining whether a goal is met, but teachers would need to plan for a pre-measure near the start of the process.

The plan to gauge success might include formal data collection methods such as exams, but it can also include information collected from checklists, classroom observations, rubrics, and other tools for formative assessment. Figure 3.4 provides an example of how a teacher might gauge success for the plan illustrated in Figure 3.3, which involves implementing writing as a tool in mathematics.

After coaching partners develop an action plan for meeting the goal and a plan for gauging success, teachers proceed to implementing the plans. During

FIGURE 3.4		
A Sample Plan for Gauging Success		
Goal: Students understand concepts and processes in unit on metric measurement, using writing as a tool.		
SUCCESS WILL LOOK LIKE/ SOUND LIKE	**TOOL FOR GAUGING SUCCESS**	**INDICATOR OF SUCCESS**
Students will write a friendly letter to someone to explain each of the difficult concepts or processes in the unit.	Students' letters	A letter written by each student exists for each of the difficult concepts or processes.
Letters written by students will include criteria for an effective explanation.	Rubric for evaluating friendly letters	Every student will receive an average total score of at least 2 on a 3-point scale.
Students will understand metric measurement concepts.	Unit exam	The average of student scores will be 20 percent higher than the average scores for the exam in the previous three years.
Students will understand metric measurement processes.	Observation checklist	Ninety percent of students will receive an average score of at least 2.5 on a 3-point scale.

this time, coaches should check in with teachers to see how things are going. At the end of the process, coaches and teachers can review the plan for gauging success and see what the information collected tells them about the action taken. At that point, they will want to determine whether the action plan was successful and should be used again, whether it should be tweaked, or whether it was ineffective. In the latter case, the coaching partners should return to the brainstormed list to seek another path to meeting the goal.

For instance, an instructional coach partnered with a middle school teacher to address the problem that students were disengaged from a civics unit on the branches of government. The teacher developed a goal that students would see how the workings of the government affected their everyday lives and then decided to try having students work in teams to research issues in the news and write to government officials about those issues. The teacher evaluated the plan in three ways: a pre- and post-questionnaire of students' attitudes and beliefs; analysis of the content of students' letters; and the unit test on branches of government. Her findings suggested that students felt more engaged with issues that mattered and believed they could influence their legislative representatives, which were desired outcomes. However, students still scored poorly on the test. The coach and teacher decided to tweak the plan by finding occasions where explicit information about the branches of government could be pointed out as the students investigated and wrote about issues; they will implement the revised plan in the following year and see how it goes.

Conclusion

Coaches help their teacher partners achieve greater success by solving problems that get in the way of success. The problem-solving cycle provides a clear path for this process and, when implemented in a coaching conversation, leads to purposeful and effective coaching partnerships. Together, coaches and teachers identify an obstacle to success, understand it, set a goal for overcoming it, develop an action plan, implement that plan, and gauge the plan's success. This cycle is illustrated in Figure 3.5.

Chapter 3 Vignette Revisited

Shaun Williams knew that he needed to find a purposeful approach to his work as a literacy coach, so he turned to online resources for coaches and began asking questions. Many coaches offered suggestions for approaches to coaching, some that he had already tried and some that seemed to have potential. A colleague pointed him in the direction of the problem-solving cycle, which Shaun studied at length and found to make sense. It took him six months to feel comfortable implementing all parts of the cycle in his coaching conversations, and he feels that it will be at least a year before he has mastered the process. However, Shaun has begun engaging teachers in the process of identifying obstacles to their success,

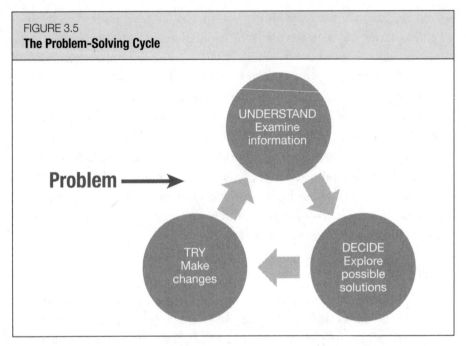

FIGURE 3.5
The Problem-Solving Cycle

Source: From *The Literacy Coach's Survival Guide: Essential Questions and Practical Answers* (2nd ed., p. 68), by C. A. Toll, 2014, Newark, DE: International Reading Association.

understanding those obstacles, and then setting a goal and trying something new as ways to address the obstacles. As a result, Shaun's coaching feels purposeful, and its direction is clear. His teacher partners seem to appreciate his guidance in moving through the problem-solving cycle. He continues to turn to colleagues, both in person and virtually, for help in enhancing his skills in bringing problem solving to life in his coaching partnerships.

4

Coaching Conversations for Implementing the Problem-Solving Cycle

> What are the characteristics of an effective coaching conversation?

> How does a coach move a conversation along?

> What is the role of the teacher in the coaching conversation?

Chapter 4 Vignette

Ariel Lindstrom has been an academic coach at Valley High School for four years. In the early years of her coaching position, Ariel focused on getting to know the teachers and the content disciplines outside her own teaching discipline of history. In the last two years, Ariel has shifted to meeting with teachers one-to-one to talk about their work. In some cases, these conversations begin with a teacher presenting an idea that she or he wants to talk about; Ariel listens as the teacher describes the situation and provides supportive statements to encourage the teacher to pursue whatever she or he has in mind. In other cases, the conversations are like pulling teeth. Ariel asks if the teacher is working on anything or wants to talk about anything, and the teacher either says "no" or brings up a topic that Ariel cannot help with. Those conversations usually are brief and then

Ariel doesn't see the teacher again. Ariel is ready to give up on conversations but doesn't know what else to do in a high school setting.

Readers who have read the first three chapters of this book likely are already interested in the coaching conversation. I hope I've been convincing about the value of the problem-solving cycle as a method for clearing away obstacles to teachers' success. Now, let's get practical about how to make it all happen in coaching conversations!

Why the Coaching Conversation?

Coaches and teachers are most likely to address matters that get in the way of teachers' success when they engage in coaching conversations. Coaching conversations are effective for several reasons:

- **They promote reflection and understanding.** As outlined in Chapter 2, when educational coaching leads teachers to greater reflection and deeper understanding, the results are longer lasting. Coaching conversations make this happen.

- **They develop relationships.** When two or more people sit side by side and talk about what matters, relationships develop. The coaching conversation is *the* best way for coaches and teachers to develop relationships.

- **They enable coaches to understand the situation.** When coaches and teachers talk about teachers' challenges, interests, and needs, coaches can listen and learn rather than assume they know all about teachers' situations. This conversation increases the likelihood that the coaches' support will be more focused and appropriate.

- **They start with teachers' perspectives, experiences, and concerns.** In coach-teacher partnerships, the teacher is the client. It's important to start with the teacher's perspective and understanding, and the coaching conversation is the ideal way to do so.

- **They honor adult learners.** Adult learners differ in what they need, how they learn, and what they expect of a coaching partnership. Coaching conversations enable coaches to tune in to the teachers they're working with and respond to the interests, pace, style, and preferences of their partners. The dance is elegant when the partners are in sync.

Key Components of the Coaching Conversation

In this section, let's look at the key components of the coaching conversation: the participants, the processes, the place, the coach's notes, data use, and the teacher's role.

The Participants

The coaching conversation is effective when working with a single teacher or a team. Coaches need a few extra skills when working with a team, which I will review in Chapter 7.

For now, to gain a better understanding of the participants in the coaching conversation—both coaches and teachers—let's address several questions that commonly arise concerning the participants.

What kind of expertise does the coach need to have? Sometimes people think that the coach has to have teaching experience at the same grade level or in the same content discipline as the teachers who participate, but that isn't the case. Remember, coaching is a partnership in which all parties contribute. Teachers in the partnership already have experience and knowledge about their content disciplines and students; the coach doesn't need the same. The best expertise for the coach to bring to the conversation is *process expertise*—that is, skill in facilitating the conversation and helping to move it along.

This isn't to say that educational coaches don't need to know anything about teaching or the content of instruction; they should have a record of successful teaching and a general awareness of the content disciplines with which they work. They can garner such awareness by reviewing curriculum documents, becoming familiar with the websites of professional organizations, attending the occasional conference in the various disciplines, and learning from colleagues. Of course, coaches with a content discipline attached to their titles, such as math specialists or literacy coaches, should have strong backgrounds in their discipline.

Who should partner with coaches? Administrators and policymakers who are not well versed in educational coaching sometimes believe that coaching is for the weakest teachers, often identified by their low student test scores. Such an approach is problematic for several reasons. First, it judges teachers on one less-than-perfect criterion. Second, it labels teachers; every teacher has strengths and areas for growth. Third, it conveys that coaching is about "fixing" flawed people when, really, it's about supporting everyone in growing strengths and solving problems. Finally, it limits the number of teachers who might want to partner with coaches, given that such a partnership would indicate that the teacher participants are weak.

Instead, coaches want to work with all kinds of teachers. However, in many situations, coaches do not have enough time to work with all teachers in a particular school. In this event, I encourage coaches to turn to their school leadership team, the team consisting of the principal and others who develop, monitor, and evaluate the school's annual goals. Members of this team likely are familiar with the school's staffing pattern, student data, and curricular content, and they can use this information to recommend a pool of teachers that might be the priority for a coach's work.

For instance, the team may recognize that certain high school content disciplines, such as social studies and English, require that students read demanding materials; therefore, it might be best for the literacy coach to work with teachers of those disciplines. Or the team may note that data indicate that the school's primary grade students have a strong foundation in math but seem to flounder in math in the intermediate grades, so teachers of those intermediate grades might be excellent coaching partners for the math specialist. Or, if the students with IEPs are placed in one house per grade level in a middle school, the team may determine that a coach's efforts should focus on those houses.

In each of these cases—where the curriculum places extra demands, where data reveal areas in which students struggle, or where students are identified as needing extra support—teaching is particularly challenging, and *that* is the message the leadership team wants to give. Rather than identifying teachers who are weak, a savvy leadership team identifies places where teachers are particularly challenged by circumstances and determines that these teachers will most benefit from a coach partner.

How effective is coaching with brand-new teachers? Educational coaches sometimes wonder whether coaching is effective with brand-new teachers. This depends on the preparation that the new teachers have received. Some educator preparation programs give preservice teachers a solid foundation, whereas others are less thorough. The only way coaches can know for sure is to have a conversation with new teachers.

If new teachers have that deer-in-the-headlights stare or have trouble answering a casual "How's it going?" without tearing up, you probably want to give them time before starting a coaching partnership. (Offering to help in other ways may be appropriate, however.) On the other hand, new teachers are ready for coaching if they explain how it's going with detail and confidence, such as, "Well, I've figured out a way to implement the science curriculum with Universal Design for Learning (UDL) concepts, but I'm still thinking about how to help my emergent bilingual students understand some of the terminology."

Are some teachers "uncoachable"? I put this term in quotation marks because it makes me uncomfortable to use it. I suppose there are people who are not up for coaching because they're in crisis in some part of their lives or are struggling with physical or mental illness. In general, though, everyone benefits from a partner who helps them think deeply about their work and how they can be more effective. Sometimes, however, a coach and potential teacher partner don't know each other well enough for the teacher to open up. Even when coaches use their best relationship-building skills (as outlined in Chapter 5), some teachers, particularly those with previous negative experiences in collaborating with colleagues, may need time to be ready to be a successful coach partner. A savvy coach will get to know such teachers in nonthreatening ways and allow those teachers to familiarize themselves with others' collaborations with the coach before inviting them into a coaching conversation.

The Processes

Most educational coaches are busy throughout every workday, expending a lot of energy making a difference in their schools. However, sometimes coaches' busyness is without direction. Coaches may respond to situations as they arise, being reactive rather than proactive, or make random attempts at helping on the basis of which teachers come to see them or who they run into in the school hallway. When these occasions arise, coaches do their best to engage their partners, but they rely on their ability to think on their feet to decide on the spot what they might say. More effective educational coaches have a plan for their coaching conversations.

The problem-solving cycle of coaching outlined in Chapter 3 is the ideal plan for coaching conversations. It begins with teachers' own interests, challenges, and perspectives and then guides them to understand their students or situation deeply, set a goal, develop a plan, implement something new in their classroom, and then look at new data to determine the effectiveness of what they tried. The cycle puts teachers in the driver's seat, with strong support in using data and other information and in being methodical about their efforts to change some aspect of their work. Harkening back to the description of models of educational coaching (see Chapter 2), one might note that the problem-solving cycle is an intellectual model that engages teachers in reflecting, learning, and planning, while at the same time assisting teachers in making practical changes to increase student learning.

"What gets in the way?" Coaches sometimes have expectations for the kinds of problems that teachers will identify for the focus of a problem-solving cycle. This may be due to a coach's existing familiarity with a teacher, the teacher's classroom, or the teacher's students. Then, when a teacher lists all the things getting in the way of success and selects one as the focus, the coach is disappointed because the problem seems superficial or more like a digression. For instance, a teacher who is not yet implementing a new curriculum, who has a classroom that feels chaotic, and who has not been using formative assessments might identify as the problem the fact that her students' lunch period comes rather late in the day and that they get hungry before that time.

I encourage coaches to go with the problem identified by their teacher partners, if at all possible. Sometimes a teacher identifies a problem that's "safe," in the sense that it won't make her vulnerable because she doesn't yet trust the coaching process. Sometimes a teacher chooses a superficial topic because he doesn't fully understand the coaching process. And at other times, the teacher doesn't yet know the coach well enough to open up about a serious issue. No matter the reason, teachers don't always choose a topic that would be the coach's choice, but that's OK.

When coaches and teachers solve a problem that is superficial or tangential to more significant issues, the following are likely to occur:

- Teachers recognize that the coaches mean what they say about being a *partner* with the teacher, not being in charge of the teacher.

- Teachers learn the problem-solving cycle.

- Trust develops between coaches and teachers.

- A problem likely is solved.

- Teachers start to recognize that partnering with a coach can make their teaching more successful.

Teachers who start their first coaching conversation with superficial topics are likely to go deeper in a second problem-solving cycle and open up much more by the third. Therefore, it's valuable to start where teachers are and continue the partnership from there so it can grow.

Sometimes teachers declare that nothing is getting in the way of their success. When this occurs, savvy coaches will listen and learn by asking further questions. I begin with a simple, "Tell me more." In some instances, my coaching partner will describe his successes and then mention an ongoing challenge. For instance, he might say, "Well, my students all go on from my class to advanced algebra, and that teacher tells me they do well. Sure, the kids with IEPs still struggle, but that's to be expected." I might then ask the teacher to tell me more about the students with IEPs—and then we have a coaching conversation! (And, by the way, I don't believe it's to be expected that students with IEPs will struggle.) I estimate that about half the time, the teachers who initially say they don't have anything getting in the way of their success subsequently talk to me about their classrooms, and we do indeed find a topic for the problem-solving cycle.

In other instances, my teacher partners respond to my request for them to tell me more by describing their rich classroom environments, effective teaching, and successful students. It's always a treat to listen to colleagues who have experienced so much success, and I take careful note of what they say for several reasons. First, I can always learn more as a teacher myself. Second, I may be working with new teachers who would benefit from partnering with successful, experienced teachers like these, and I often will follow up by asking if I can refer those new teachers to them. In addition, teachers who are highly successful are often investigating new areas for growth and change.

For instance, I may hear from one of these teachers that she's interested in bringing the arts into her classroom, and I may be aware that another teacher in the same school would like to do the same. I love being a matchmaker to folks like these. Or I may listen to a teacher describe her next endeavor and offer to partner with her; thus, a coaching partnership is formed, not to solve a problem but to pursue a common interest whose purpose is still to enhance teacher success.

In a small number of cases, when teachers tell me that nothing is getting in the way of their success, they're probably covering up their struggles due to embarrassment. I suspect this is the case if a teacher is unable to describe his success in any detail. When I ask him to tell me more, he may say, "Oh, the students are all doing really well." Then, when I ask him to describe what the students are learning and how he knows, he might say, "They're just working hard and trying their best. I just can tell." And so it continues; no matter how I probe, no substantive information is shared. In cases such as this, I don't give up on the teacher. Rather, I ask if it's OK to check back in a couple weeks, and I do. I continue to check in with the teacher until a conversation opens up.

Understanding. When coaches and teachers deepen their understanding of a problem, a lot of information emerges. As coaches ask questions of teachers to further understanding, they likely jot down teachers' responses, which is a good tactic. And if coaches and teachers engage in learning to find answers to some of those questions, one or both likely will keep notes.

However, keeping track of all the information garnered can sometimes be a challenge. Coaches can help teachers mentally organize information about a problem in several ways:

- **By sorting.** Look for clusters of similar items. For instance, if a teacher is struggling to get the entire class to complete their writing assignments, as the coach and teacher come to understand the problem further, they may recognize that some students are failing to finish because they lack stamina, others are getting lost in the writing process, a few just don't care, and several are unsure about what they want to say. This clustering enables the coach and teacher to recognize that there are actually four problems, not one, and to seek ways to resolve the issues presented by each subgroup of students.

- **By comparing.** Sometimes a metaphor captures an essential characteristic of a situation. For instance, a coach working with a new teacher who was feeling overwhelmed listened as she described her attempt to focus on four groups of students simultaneously: those who were challenged by the course, those who sought advanced study, those who struggled with English, and those with IEPs. The coach said, "It seems like you're a firefighter at a burning house. Just as you get the flames quelled in one area, they flare up in another, and you rush from one part of the house to another." This resonated with the teacher and enabled her to accept that she was indeed trying to solve multiple challenges at once. She teared up but also expressed appreciation that the coach understood her situation.

- **By visualizing.** Coaches can help teachers work with the information garnered by making it visual, using stick figures, arrows, keywords, charts, or other quickly sketched images. For instance, when I'm in coaching conversations, I often draw stick figures to represent my understanding of what my teacher partners are describing. Recently, a special education resource teacher explained to me the different expectations and styles of the four classrooms in which she worked, as well as the challenges she faced in being in such diverse settings. I quickly sketched boxes for the four classrooms she described, drew a stick figure for each of her teacher colleagues, and then used arrows and keywords to represent her relationship to each classroom and teacher. The visual helped me make sure I understood correctly and gave us a reference point as our conversation continued.

Coaches and teachers who are trying to understand a situation thoroughly will engage in a process that may take one full session or several coaching sessions. Just as it's important to build a house with a strong foundation, taking the time to understand a problem before solving it is well worth the effort.

Deciding. Teachers and coaches sometimes describe an action instead of a goal. For instance, a teacher might say that his goal is for all his students to create a web page for a science unit on ecology. However, creating a web page is an activity, not a goal. Rather, the goal may be that students will understand key concepts from ecology; then they might use the web page to show they understand those concepts.

One way coaches can help teachers think about goals is to suggest that a goal describes how someone—in this case, the teacher or students—will be different as a result of an action plan. In the case of the unit on ecology, the students will be different because they understand concepts about ecology. True, the students may be different as a result of creating a web page, especially if it's their first attempt at such a project, but that's not the purpose of teaching the unit. The goal of the unit is understanding ecological concepts.

Sometimes when brainstorming how to meet the goal, a step in this phase of the problem-solving cycle, coaches have many ideas for possible actions, and teachers have few or none. Now, I believe that coaches should always be authentic and honest, but in this one situation, I suggest that coaches hold back a little. Consider the opposite: If a coach comes forth with 5, 8, or 10 ideas and the teacher sits in silence, the teacher may conclude that the coach should just have told her what to do in the first place. The process becomes disempowering for teachers and reinforces the mistaken idea that coaches are hired to tell teachers what to do. Instead, coaches should suggest just one idea more than their teacher partners. So, if a teacher has two ideas for how to meet the goal, a coach will suggest no more than three. If there aren't enough ideas generated between the partners, coaches and teachers can turn to resources to learn more and come up with more possibilities.

Coaches sometimes wonder whether the goals developed by their teacher partners must be SMART goals, meaning the goals are specific, measurable, achievable, relevant, and time-bound (Doran, 1981). There's nothing wrong with developing such a goal, but it's often cumbersome for teachers to do so. In addition, the term *measurable* always gives me pause, because although goals should be able to be evaluated, some goals don't lend themselves to measurement. For instance, a teacher's goal of providing a productive learning environment for the entire class while she conferences with individual students might be evaluated using a checklist of observable behavior without putting a number on the behaviors observed. My advice is to work toward goals that are appropriate for solving the problems identified and that are worth the investment of teachers' time and to focus on the other characteristics only if one's teacher partners choose to do so.

Trying. The Trying phase of the problem-solving cycle usually goes smoothly. After all, most teachers are experienced at planning and trying new things. However, coaches occasionally find that their partners don't actually do what they said they were going to do. For instance, a coach may check back with a team of three teachers who committed to trying some new vocabulary instructional strategies and find that none of the teachers did so. I encourage coaches in these situations to delve deeper. A good question is, "When you think about [implementing the actions that were planned], what's getting in the way?" Commonly, whatever has gotten in the way is temporary, such as a teacher's illness or an unexpected requirement from an administrator. However, occasionally the issue that gets in the way is significant and in itself becomes the focus of the problem-solving cycle. For instance, if a teacher identifies that what's getting in the way of her plan to teach about opioid abuse is her inability to find time in the day, then the coach and teacher can tackle that problem before returning to the original action plan.

Coaches can make good use of the plan for implementation (see the sample action plan shown in Figure 3.3) to identify places where teacher partners may be particularly challenged and to check in with them around that time. Similarly, coaches can use the plan to evaluate whether the problem is solved (see the sample plan for gauging success shown in Figure 3.4) by using it for follow-up conversations. For instance, if a teacher determines that one piece of evidence will be students' scores on a project, the coach may suggest that they look at the scores to consider the effectiveness of the plan. In this way, coaches and teachers develop routines of looking for evidence of progress.

The Place

The location of a coaching conversation can make a difference in its effectiveness. Savvy coaches ensure that they meet with their teacher partners in a quiet place where they will not be interrupted for at least 30 minutes if only one teacher is involved or for 45 to 60 minutes if the conversation is with a team. It's usually ideal to meet in a teacher's classroom when no students are present. Then, if the teacher needs a calendar, a sample of student work, a textbook, assessment data, or something else, it's likely nearby. It's important for students not to be present so teachers can focus on the conversation and to ensure privacy. Should a teacher suggest meeting in his classroom when students are working on a project or reading silently, wise coaches ask for another meeting time.

The Coach's Notes

Coaches should take notes of their coaching conversations. Here are some items to include:

- Date of meeting

- Names of those present

- Topics discussed

- Goals set (if appropriate)

- Decisions made (if appropriate)

- Next steps

- Next meeting date, time, and location

Notes serve several purposes. They help coaches remember the details of every coaching conversation, a helpful resource for all coaches and a necessity for those of us who are very busy or in later middle age. Notes also provide teachers with a record of the coaching conversation, which may assist them in noting any actions they have committed to and reminding them of the next meeting. Notes also provide a record over time of a coaching partnership; some coaches and teachers work together for years, whether continuously or in cycles, and often they want to revisit earlier decisions or items discussed.

Coaches should not share notes from their coaching conversations with principals or other supervisors. If administrators wish to know what occurs during coaching partnerships, they certainly can ask the teachers involved, but they should not put coaches on the spot for reporting on teachers. (More on this in Chapter 8.)

Some coaches struggle to organize notes. Many coaches find it helps to have a large binder with a section for each teacher or team with whom the coach works. In each section, coaches place notes from coaching conversations, copies of resources shared, and anything else that would be helpful. These days, technology provides ways to create virtual "binders" in which the same kind of information can be located. I encourage coaches to consider going the technological route for the convenience of having all their notes at their fingertips.

Data Use

The problem-solving cycle usually benefits from data use, and the coaching conversation usually assists teachers in using data well. However, there's a place for data in the conversation—and it's not at the start. This is contrary to the beliefs of many administrators and some coaches, who believe that the coaching conversation should begin by presenting teachers with data and then asking teachers to identify a problem based on those data. Such an approach is problematic for several reasons:

- **It assumes that data motivate people.** They don't. Think about when you decided to become a teacher. Did you tell your folks, "I want to teach because I want to make data-driven decisions"? Of course not. You wanted to teach because you cared about kids or you cared about your subject discipline.

- **It assumes that people are good at data-driven decision making.** Actually, we aren't. There's evidence that people make decisions and then find data to justify those decisions. Watch yourself or your colleagues, and you'll notice this impulse. Too often, we decide that a student should have an IEP or that a colleague should teach at a different grade level and then we mentally collect the data to prove our point.

- **It leads teachers to "do data" rather than "think data."** Let me explain by providing a comparison. Back in the 1990s, when the only computers in a school were in a computer lab, teachers and students stopped everything they were doing, usually once a week, and went to the lab to "do computers." What happened in the lab was rarely connected to what happened during the rest of the day. Today, teachers and students usually have computers in the form of laptops, tablets, or computers on wheels (COWs) right in the classroom. Throughout the day, computer technology supports other kinds of learning. Similarly, when teachers rely on data coaches, data walls, or administrators' presentation of data, they usually attend to data apart from the rest of their planning, reflection, and problem solving. Looking at data becomes an event, as teachers "do data" for the purpose of starting a coaching conversation.

Instead, I want teachers to "think data" by routinely relying on data multiple times every day. I want teachers to feel that they would be as stymied in their work if they did not have data as they would be if they didn't have a computer or laptop in their classroom.

So how do data fit into the coaching conversation? Data are essential tools for every part of the problem-solving cycle, except, as I have noted, the beginning. In the Understanding phase, data help teachers and coaches gain a clearer picture of the situation, student, or curricular component. In the Deciding phase, data inform teachers' goal development and can influence what teachers decide to do to reach the goal. For instance, let's say that a teacher has developed a goal that students who are English language learners will comprehend what they read in their history textbook; after looking at the data on the students' writing achievement, the teacher may decide against a possible action item that involves teaching those students to write summaries of each chapter. Finally, data are used in the Trying phase of the problem-solving cycle to inform teachers and coaches of the effect of what was implemented, which can then help them determine whether to continue with the action, tweak it, or eliminate it.

When it comes to accessing, analyzing, and using data, educational coaches sometimes take on responsibility for all of these tasks. When data are needed, coaches track them down. When data are complex, coaches spend time parsing and disaggregating the information. When it is time to think about the significance of data, coaches share their insights with teachers. In many cases, coaches are providing a real service to their schools and their colleagues when they engage in such practices. However, I'd like to nudge coaches to think about teaching others to do the data work themselves. When coaches apprise teachers about where data can be found, how to analyze data, and the significance of data, they build teachers' capacity. That's coaching at its best!

The Teacher's Role in the Coaching Conversation

Teachers are often unfamiliar with coaching conversations. Even those who have worked with coaches before sometimes worked within a model of coaching that did not engage partners in an equal relationship. Therefore, wise coaches provide some information upfront to teachers so they know what to expect.

A good way to do so is to talk to teachers at an all-faculty or all-staff meeting. Even if coaches are not working with every teacher in the building, it helps if all teachers understand a bit about coaching. Of course, one really doesn't understand coaching until one participates in a coaching partnership, but an explanation can be a good start.

Teachers usually want to know what coaching is all about in general, how the particular coach or coaches in their school will work, and the effect coaching will have on them. Coaches usually want teachers to understand their role in coaching conversations and how the teachers can optimize their partnership with a coach. To assist in these areas, I provide two sample handouts. Figure 4.1

FIGURE 4.1

Sample Handout: The Basics of Educational Coaching

What? Job-embedded professional development

Why? To enhance your success

How? Through a problem-solving partnership

What will a meeting with the coach be like?
One-to-one: We will meet for 30 minutes at a time. The coach will start out by asking you what gets in the way of your students' learning and your teaching, and after brainstorming, you will pick one topic you'd like to focus on. Then you and the coach will work through a process to eliminate or lessen that problem.

Teams: The coach will work with the teams to determine how often she might facilitate coaching conversations and how she can best partner with team members to implement the problem-solving cycle.

Is the coach going to tell me what to do?
The coach is your partner in reflection, problem solving, and decision making. The coach will provide expertise about how to make the process go smoothly, and you will provide expertise about your students and your curriculum. You will be the decision maker when it comes to the focus of the conversations, the goals you set, and the action steps you might take.

Does working with a coach mean I am a poor teacher?
To the contrary, engagement in a coaching partnership demonstrates your commitment and professionalism. We all can benefit from having a coach partner.

Will this affect my evaluation?
The coach has nothing to do with your evaluation and does not discuss you with your supervisor. However, you may want to share what you are learning in the coaching partnership with your supervisor as evidence of your continued growth and success. But that decision is up to you.

FIGURE 4.2
Sample Handout: The Teacher's Role in the Coaching Conversation

Understand
- Learn about coaching and the coach's role.
- Get to know the coach—as a person and a teacher.
- Know the overall aim of the coaching program.

Prepare
- Think about how to make the best use of the time devoted to the coaching conversation.
- Focus your preparations on problems you'd like to solve or interests you'd like to pursue, rather than seeking solutions in advance of the conversation. (Seeking solutions is a big part of the coaching relationship!)
- Gather evidence that may be useful in the conversation—for example, samples of student work, summaries of student assessments, or teaching materials you'd like to use.
- Arrive at the meeting with the coach on time and ready to give it your full attention.

Communicate
- Recognize that the coaching conversation requires active participation of all members.
- Seek to describe rather than complain, forecast, or demand.
- Ask about anything that isn't clear:
  - The content of the conversation
  - The process of coaching
- Assume the coach sincerely wants to know what you have to say.

Follow Through
- Review notes from the conversation.
- Attend to any information gathering you committed to in the conversation.
- Think about furthering the conversation in your next meeting.

---

shows a handout for teachers that explains the basics of coaching. Figure 4.2 shows a handout for teachers that explains their role in the process.

Conclusion

The coaching conversation is the best way to implement a problem-solving model of coaching. Coaches can assist teachers in achieving greater success by helping teachers identify an obstacle, understand the problem more deeply, set a goal for resolving the problem, develop a plan to try something to meet the goal, and evaluate their actions to determine whether the problem is solved or whether to continue working on it. With time and practice, coaches will finesse their ability to facilitate the coaching conversation in ways that optimize teachers' reflection, learning, and growth.

Chapter 4 Vignette Revisited

Before giving up on the idea of having meaningful coaching conversations with teachers at her high school, Ariel Lindstrom got some help in learning how to implement a problem-solving cycle as the substance of her coaching conversations. She now asks the teachers to identify something getting in the way of their success or their students' success and helps them understand those challenges, set goals, and implement something new to meet the goals. She also helps the teachers determine whether what they have tried is effective or whether they need to try something else. In these ways, she finds her coaching conversations to be smoother and more meaningful, but above all, she finds that the conversations support teachers in solving problems and increasing their success.

5

Developing Coaching Partnerships

> What kind of relationship should coaches have with teachers?

> How do coaches develop partnerships?

> How can coaches best use their connectivity, acceptance, and trustworthiness?

> How can coaches put their best foot forward in a coaching role?

Chapter 5 Vignette

Sandra Coleman is in her second year as a literacy coach at Washington Elementary School. She taught 1st grade in the school for seven years, so she knew the teachers well when she began her work as a coach. Sandra has learned the value of coaching conversations, so she regularly meets with teachers to talk about what's going on in their classrooms and to inquire about any struggles the teachers are having. Sandra is proud of her successful teaching background and sees herself as generous in sharing her insight and experience with others. When teachers present a problem to her, Sandra usually has two or three ideas to help, and when she doesn't, she researches the problem and gets back to teachers quickly.

Despite her pride in this approach, Sandra has become worried. She notices that a few teachers often come to her for assistance in a manner that feels a bit dependent. As for the other teachers, fewer and fewer of them initiate conversations with her; she usually has to approach them. Also, she has noticed that many of the teachers she has worked with are not using some of the strategies that she taught them in their first year together. She thought she was making a difference, but now she's not so sure.

Educational coaching is a relationship that includes a coach and one or more teachers. Different coaches understand the nature of that relationship differently. In my study of coaching, I find that the coach can play any of the following roles:

- Supervisor: The coach oversees teachers, making sure they implement programs and use recommended practices.

- Technician: The coach offers advice and provides demonstrations to teachers.

- Cheerleader: The coach encourages teachers.

- Helper: The coach lends a hand to teachers whenever needed.

- Captain: The coach leads teachers in developing and implementing programs and curricula.

These roles are important in schools. However, before the implementation of coaching, teachers had already experienced these kinds of relationships. That is, there have always been people who encourage, supervise, lead, help, and provide technical advice in schools. It is not a good use of resources to create educational coaching positions in which coaches replicate what already exists. In fact, when this occurs, it is usually because the people who are *supposed to* lead, help, encourage, supervise, or provide technical assistance are not doing their jobs. Hiring someone else is not the best approach to correcting a lax or misguided employee.

Coaching Partnerships

A better relationship to develop is the coaching partnership. This is not a relationship that many teachers have previously experienced, and it is one that helps tremendously. Think about a ballroom dance in which the lead directs his partner with a light touch on the shoulder or back, and the partner follows in sync. Similarly, coaches lead teachers in partnerships but with the lightest touch, and they must be in sync. Too much direction from a dancer or coach and the partnership becomes forced; too little direction and the partners are at loose ends, likely going in different directions.

For dance partners or coach partners to do well together, the lead must pay close attention to his partner and must make small but important adjustments as they move along. Both partners need to be committed to the dance, whether it is an elegant glide across the ballroom floor or an engaged cycle of educator problem solving. And neither the ballroom dance nor the coaching partnership happens by magic; it takes effort and skill, which is what this book is about.

In Chapter 1, I introduced the qualities of Connectivity, Acceptance, and being Trustworthy as essentials for successful coaching. CAT qualities are essential because partnerships will not develop without them. Here are some ways to use these qualities in establishing partnerships.

Connectivity

Connecting with coaching partners is about finding a Goldilocks zone of being neither too lax in reaching out to teachers nor too forceful. Some coaches make the mistake of waiting for teachers to take the initial steps toward connection and then "going with the goers," as the saying goes. The teachers with whom coaches then work have expressed interest in working with them by asking for their help. There are problems with this approach, though. It positions the coach as the passive recipient of teachers' interest. It likely supports teachers who either are already collaborative or teachers who are looking for someone to lean on. And it ignores all the other teachers in the building!

Savvy educational coaches will initiate connections with teachers by approaching them. It is best for all teachers in a school to work with a coach. However, there are often more teachers than a coach or coaches can reasonably work with; in that case, I suggest that administrators identify a pool of teachers working in particularly challenging situations, a process I discuss in Chapter 8.

Many coaches establish partnerships with teachers by scheduling a regular meeting with them as individuals or with their teams. For instance, coaches and teachers might have a standing appointment to meet every two weeks. In this way, the coaching partnership is solidified because coaches and teachers connect regularly.

Some coaches and teachers prefer what I call "the wave," in which coaches tune in to teachers' priorities and needs and schedule flexibly. For instance, a coach may schedule weekly meetings for new teachers but wait two months before meeting with a team of teachers in the same school that may be working on a project that does not require the coach's involvement. Such flexible scheduling requires that coaches are well organized and that they really understand the needs of their teacher partners. This approach works for some coaches but not all.

When I mentioned the Goldilocks point of connectivity, I implied that coaches can work too hard to connect with teachers, and that is true. If teachers express hesitation about partnering, wise coaches will find a middle space where they give teachers some breathing room but do not give up on them. I find that checking back in two weeks is a good span of time if an initial connection does not occur.

Acceptance

A key to developing partnerships is avoiding judgment. We humans would like to believe that we are skilled at thinking one thing and behaving in an opposite way, as when we might judge a person negatively but speak and act as though we are accepting of them. However, much of the time we provide potential partners with subtle clues—a slight turn of the shoulder, a tightening around the mouth, a change in the tone of voice—that reveal our inner thoughts and feelings. It is much better to avoid judging in the first place.

The best way to avoid judging is to be centered in the present moment. When coaches are present to what is occurring at the very moment, they tune in to their perceptions—particularly what they see in and hear from their partner—and respond accordingly. Judging usually arises when one is concerned about what has happened or will happen or when one focuses on others' opinions, such as when a coach worries that a teacher will repeat a previous mistake or ponders whether a colleague will frown on an idea being discussed. Coaches who practice staying present—and it does require practice!—will quiet their judging minds and will automatically convey acceptance to their partners.

A perspective that also helps is that of assuming good intentions. In my work with thousands of teachers over the years, I have met only one who I believe did not care about students. Teachers go to school every day with a commitment to doing good work and making a difference. Like all humans, we teachers have moments and even days when we are not at our best, and sometimes at those moments we reveal frustration, anger, worry, or distraction. But people are good and, in my book, teachers as a group are a little better than good! When coaches approach all colleagues with an understanding that they have good intentions, a partnership is much more likely to form.

Trust

Sometimes coaches believe that trust must exist for a partnership to move forward. However, the opposite is true. To understand how trust develops in a partnership, it may be helpful to reflect on partnerships you have outside of your workday. Think about your relationship with your spouse or significant other, with a best friend, or with a co-chair on a committee in a civic club or at your church, mosque, or temple. You likely trust that person, and that trust likely developed as you dated, enjoyed mutual hobbies, planned fundraisers, or engaged in some other endeavor. Trust develops when one is trustworthy. Therefore, coaches who collaborate will develop trust. Of course, one must also be trustworthy in that collaboration. I provide tips for trustworthy communication in Chapter 6.

A Partnership Pitfall: Telling Teachers What to Do

A common assumption among school administrators and policymakers is that educational coaches enact tasks that are similar to those performed by teachers' supervisors, but without the threat of evaluation. For instance, many school principals tell educational coaches to begin their work by observing teachers in their classrooms, deciding what teachers need to do to improve, and then meeting with teachers to explain what they, the coaches, think the teachers should do. This focus on teachers' behaviors is a limited view of how teaching changes over the long term. In addition, it suggests a role for educational coaches that is often counterproductive.

When coaches determine what teachers need, explain or demonstrate it, and then help teachers to change as the coaches have prescribed, they do the thinking for teachers, thus robbing teachers of opportunities to increase their skills in understanding obstacles to their success and how to overcome them.

It is human nature to resist being told what to do by others, particularly others with whom we do not have a relationship and who are making decisions about something we really care about, and this is true of teachers when coaches attempt to direct their actions. Conversely, when teachers *want* coaches to tell them what to do, coaches who take this approach reinforce those teachers' dependence and impede the teachers' own development as problem solvers and decision makers.

I have developed a visual, shown in Figure 5.1, that illustrates the potential pitfalls of coaching-as-telling.

FIGURE 5.1
When a Coach Gives Advice

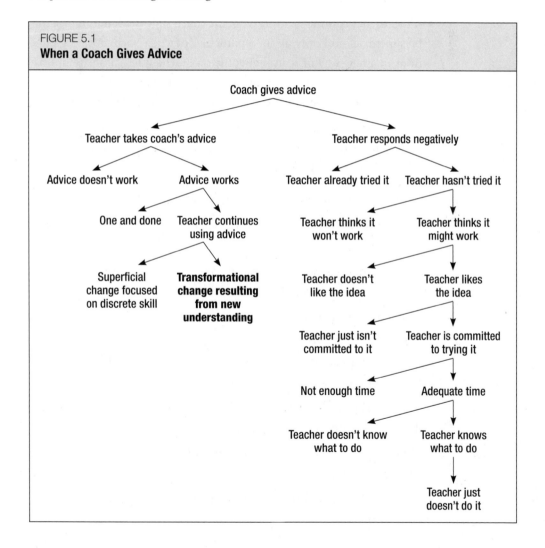

How Teachers Will React

When a coach tells a teacher what to do, the teacher may either take the advice or respond negatively. First, let's look at what may happen if the teacher takes the advice:

- The advice may or may not work.

- If the advice works, the teacher may use it only once and then forget about it (one and done).

- If the teacher continues doing what the coach suggested, the change may be superficial and only about a particular practice, such as giving directions in a new way or rearranging the daily schedule. These are not bad changes, but they are not transformative in a manner that will lead to significant improvements in teachers' effectiveness and student learning.

- If the teacher continues doing what the coach suggested, the change may be transformative in altering the teacher's understanding and decision making. This is the outcome desired from coaching.

In other cases, the teacher may respond negatively:

- The teacher may have already tried what the coach advised and found it ineffective.

- If the teacher has not tried what the coach suggested, the teacher may believe it won't work and therefore will not try it.

- If the teacher believes the suggestion might work, she may not like it and therefore will ignore it.

- If the teacher likes the suggestion, he may not be committed to making the change at this time.

- If the teacher feels committed to the suggested change, she may find that she does not have enough time.

- If the teacher does have enough time to implement the suggested change, he may not know how to do it.

- If the teacher knows how to implement the change, she may simply decide not to try it.

In this series of possibilities, only one is desired: a transformational change that results from teachers' enhanced understanding and decision making. This is the only option that justifies the time and cost of educational coaching. As we can see, such a change might result from a coach telling a teacher what to do. But look at all the other possibilities! There are many less-than-desired results that may come from telling teachers what to do, demonstrating the risks and likelihood of failure that come from that strategy. There are better practices, such as using the problem-solving model of coaching.

That Urge to Give Advice

Before moving on, I'd like to consider the phenomenon of coaches' urge to give advice. It is strong. Even coaches with advanced training who know all the reasons why advice giving is not the wisest tactic still find themselves engaging in this practice. I understand how easily coaches fall into this trap, considering who becomes an educational coach.

In general, teachers are asked to be educational coaches because they have a history of success in their own classrooms. Thus, they are skilled and insightful. Also, teachers who are invited to become educational coaches usually do so because they want to help. So we have skilled practitioners who want to be helpful—a perfect storm for advice giving! Coaches want to make a difference, and they engaged in effective teaching practices themselves, which leads them to want to give advice about what to do. In addition, offering suggestions makes coaches quickly appear helpful—to both teachers and themselves. When coaches use other more thoughtful tactics, their effectiveness may not be evident for some time, even though that effectiveness is usually greater and more lasting.

By the way, I perceive the irony that in this book I give advice to coaches despite my understanding of the limitations of advice giving. In fact, I am well aware that there are better ways for me to influence educational coaches than advising them in a book, and I engage in those better ways when I am able to have a partnership with the coaches with whom I work. Unfortunately, the limitations of communicating in writing and at a distance include the fact that suggestions, insight, and information are mostly what I can provide here. My wish is that these ideas will create awareness and initiative for coaches to begin enhancing their practice and then reflect and partner for further growth.

Bringing Your Best Self to the Coaching Partnership

Anyone who has been in a romantic relationship or good friendship understands the importance of bringing your best self to the partnership. Note that I didn't say *perfect self*—none of us would have a relationship if that were required! However, offering our partners the kind, funny, fair, and smart parts of ourselves most of the time is important. Here are a few tips for doing so in a coaching partnership.

Listen

Listening is the first task of coaching. Listen. Enough said.

Develop Comfort in Your Role

Most people who are selected to serve as coaches have become skilled teachers, so it can be jarring to step out of a role in which one was experiencing success into a new role where one is on shakier ground. True, coaches draw on their teaching experience and are still committed to students' success, but the coaching role requires many different skills.

It might help to recall one's first year as a teacher. Most of us get a little uncomfortable thinking about the missteps of that first year. My purpose in mentioning it is twofold: First, you and the students survived, and second, you learned and grew. Similarly, you and the teachers you work with will survive any blunders you make in the first years of coaching, and you likely will grow into a skilled and successful coach.

Even experienced coaches are sometimes uncomfortable in their role. Now, it could be that coaching is just not for them, and that is nothing to worry about. Most coaches can return to teaching in their own classrooms, and how lucky their future students will be if that is a decision they make. However, in many cases coaches who remain uncomfortable in their roles have not had the support and professional development they need. In Chapter 8, I discuss working with administrators who are not entirely clear about or supportive of coaching, but here I'd like to stress the importance of your own professional development.

Learning to coach effectively *does* require learning. Of course, if you are reading this book, you're interested in advancing your coaching skills. Beyond reading books, articles, and online resources, coaches benefit from having a network of support. In large school districts, such support often comes from the district's own leadership and from the collaboration among coaches in the district. If you are in such a district and the coaches are *not* meeting as a group for at least one afternoon a month, I encourage you to initiate collaborative efforts.

In school districts without a large coaching cadre, coaches may feel more isolated. If you are in such a district, bear in mind that there are probably other isolated coaches in your region. Turn to an organization or agency and ask them to sponsor a coach network. In the United States, organizations that are receptive to such a request include Boards of Cooperative Educational Services (BOCES); Regional Offices of Education (ROEs); Cooperative Educational Services Agencies (CESAs); Education Service Districts (ESDs); Area Education Agencies (AEAs); or other organizations, depending on the state. Local, state, or provincial councils of the International Literacy Association or the National Council of Teachers of Mathematics also may support development of a coach network. The point is, don't go it alone.

Accept Limits on Your Control

Many educational coaches are passionately committed to their work and their schools. Sometimes, in their dedication to making a contribution, coaches start feeling overly responsible and actually become less effective as a result. Recognizing what one does and doesn't control is a good step in bringing one's best self to the partnership. Here are some common areas where coaches need to accept limits on their control.

When a teacher makes a "wrong" decision. One place where control is sometimes an issue is when teachers make decisions that would not be the coach's choice. For instance, a teacher with students struggling to read the textbook might develop study guides for each chapter, whereas the coach would choose alternate texts. Wise coaches recognize that there usually is more than one way to succeed as a teacher. In addition, the problem-solving cycle includes collecting data about actions taken, so if a teacher makes a decision that is not effective, there will be opportunity to note it as such and try something different.

When a teacher persistently struggles. Coaches may become aware of a teacher colleague who is failing to create a productive learning environment, failing to implement the curriculum, or failing to provide even minimally effective instruction. In such cases, coaches are sometimes tempted to take action beyond inviting such teachers into a partnership. It is important for coaches to remember, though, that they are *not* those teachers' supervisor, and that it's the supervisor's responsibility to intervene when a teacher truly is in trouble.

Sometimes coaches believe that supervisors are not taking action. However, if a supervisor is involved appropriately, coaches shouldn't be aware of this because, as coaches, they should not be privy to such confidential personnel matters. Sometimes coaches believe that supervisors are ignorant about effective teaching or about what's happening in the classroom. This is usually not the case, but in those rare instances where a supervisor is not performing well, the responsibility for correcting the situation rests with the supervisor's supervisor, not the coach.

When it comes to sharing one's vision. Another area in which coaches sometimes assume too much control concerns the vision for the particular program, department, team, or school in which they work. This error may be the result of a popular piece of advice given to managers: Share your vision. Now, perhaps it is appropriate for leaders in some industries to create and share their vision as a way to strengthen the organization, but it is not an effective strategy for coaches. As Sam Chaltain (2009) points out, wise school leaders *find* the vision of those in the school. Similarly, coaches' role in relation to vision is to support others in developing their vision. Of course, coaches can contribute as members of the school staff, but they will push their partners away if they assume that their vision alone should become the prevailing one.

Be Comfortable in Your Own Skin

Occasionally, coaches won't bring their best selves to the role because they're not in touch with their best selves. We are all on our individual paths in life, and for some, the path is rougher than others, which can sometimes impede people from being comfortable with who they are and sharing that self with others. Helping coaches transition to healthy self-regard is beyond the scope of this book or my abilities. I do encourage readers who recognize themselves in this description to turn to a trusted other for support.

Recently my church called a new minister. When she was at a getting-to-know-you event, she shared two themes that resonate in her ministry: It's not about you, and you are enough. I have thought a lot about these concepts. Because we humans can only perceive the world through our own experiences, we so often see ourselves at the center and make everything about us. This reminder may be helpful to coaches who might feel too visible, central, or essential to the work in schools. You are only part of the team, albeit a valuable part.

Regarding the second idea, that one is enough, we humans sometimes fall into the trap of questioning whether we are worthy. As coaches, we may doubt that we are the right people to serve in visible leadership roles in schools. Coaches may benefit from reflecting on the qualities they bring to their role and the continued efforts they make to grow those qualities, especially connectivity, acceptance, and trustworthiness. It can be helpful to bear in mind the previous point, that it's not all about any one of us, because it reminds us that responsibility does not just rest on coaches' shoulders. In collaboration, we all bring something of worth, and we benefit from the best selves that our colleagues put forward as well.

Conclusion

When coaches resist the urge to tell teachers what to do; when they consider their work with teachers to be a partnership; when they are attentive, receptive, and trustworthy; and when they bring their best selves to their work, they create optimal partnerships for enhancing teachers' success.

Chapter 5 Vignette Revisited

Sandra Coleman decided to talk to someone about her concerns that her positive start with teachers was waning in the third year of her coaching experience. She turned to Vanessa, her school district's curriculum coordinator, who was also the supervisor of literacy coaches in the elementary schools and was a former coach herself. Vanessa and Sandra met several times, which enabled Vanessa to listen carefully to Sandra's description of her efforts and their outcomes. Vanessa helped Sandra dig deeper into the challenges she was facing and arranged for Sandra to shadow two other coaches in the district. Vanessa then helped Sandra to set a goal and develop a plan to meet the goal.

Sandra's goal was to create a new approach to coaching conversations based on her shadowing observations and her realization—much to Vanessa's delight—that Vanessa herself was engaging Sandra in a coach-the-coach conversation that felt very different from the ones Sandra was conducting with teachers. She realized that both the coaches she shadowed and Vanessa herself did not provide solutions but rather facilitated a process that enabled their partners in the coaching conversation (teachers and, in Vanessa's case, Sandra) to understand and solve their own problems.

Over time, Sandra developed skill in facilitating problem solving rather than giving solutions, and she found that it transformed not only the nature of her coaching conversations, but also the impact she had in her school. Now in her fifth year as a literacy coach at Washington Elementary, Sandra sees that teachers have learned and changed as a result of the coaching partnerships they have with her, and those changes persist across years.

6

Communication for Partnering and Problem Solving

> How can I make CAT coach qualities visible in my partnerships?

> What kinds of questions facilitate the coaching partnership?

> How can coaches best respond to unpleasant comments?

Chapter 6 Vignette

Andre Brooks believed that he was an excellent coach. He was friendly to everyone and did his best to reserve judgment of his teacher colleagues. He met with each of his teacher partners for coaching conversations in which they implemented a problem-solving cycle to increase teacher effectiveness. During those conversations, Andre asked a lot of questions and attempted to listen carefully. However, the coaching conversations often seemed to fall flat. The conversations began well enough, with Andre's coaching partners identifying a problem impeding their success, but Andre had difficulty getting teachers to go in depth or work on solving problems. After two years of attempting these conversations, Andre was worried he had chosen the wrong job.

It's no secret that educators must be good communicators, and that's certainly the case for educational coaches. In many ways, communication is *the* job of educational coaches because communication is the basis for any effective partnership, be it a partnership between spouses, business colleagues, or coaches and teachers. As the framework for helping coaches enhance their communication skills, I return in this chapter to the CAT essential qualities of Connectivity, Acceptance, and Trustworthiness.

Communication for Connection

Partners must make a connection in order to collaborate, and that's certainly true of coaching partnerships. Educational coaches can engage in specific actions to communicate connection with teacher partners. Some suggestions follow.

"What Gets in the Way?"

The question I presented in Chapter 4 as the starting point for the coaching conversation—*When you think about the learning you want your students to do and the teaching you want to do, what gets in the way?*—promotes connection. It inquires into the teachers' vision for what they want to occur in their classrooms and the obstacles to success. It positions the teacher at the center of the partnership and the coach as the person who supports the teacher in problem finding and problem solving. When coaches ask this question, they demonstrate interest in their teacher partners and create an opportunity to learn more.

Paraphrasing

Paraphrasing serves two purposes: It provides evidence that one is listening and ensures that one has heard accurately. Both further connectivity. When coaches paraphrase, they don't merely repeat what their partner has said but, rather, they put what their partner has said into their own words. An effective paraphrase includes key words that the teacher partner has used and demonstrates that the coach understands what was said. Figure 6.1 provides several examples that demonstrate how coaches might use paraphrasing to check for understanding, as well as to show understanding; they ask for confirmation that they paraphrased the information correctly using questions such as, "Did I get that right?" and "Is that accurate?"

FIGURE 6.1
Examples of Effective Paraphrasing

Teacher: One of my concerns about Mia is that she seems to understand science but has no interest in it.

Coach: I hear you that you're concerned about Mia's lack of interest in science, even though she understands it.

Teacher: This unit always confuses students. For starters, they seem to have a hard time understanding the concept of a negative integer.

Coach: One of the confusing things about this unit is that students don't understand the concept of a negative integer. Did I get that right?

Teacher: My students are very selective about reading poetry. They like poems that rhyme and are funny, but their eyes glaze over when I try to transition to free verse or poems on serious topics.

Coach: I understand that your students are interested in funny poems and rhyming poems, but they lose interest when poems are unrhymed or not funny. Is that accurate?

Digging Deeper

Coaches who connect well with teachers encourage them to explain their situations, students, and dilemmas using prompts such as, "Say some more about that, please" and "Could you tell me more?" Coaches display genuine curiosity about learning more, and, in the process, teachers reflect further on the situation. The coaches' requests to tell more are open-ended, enabling them to learn without setting the direction.

Figure 6.2 includes examples of ineffective as well as effective probing. Note that in the "ineffective" example, the coach leads the conversation and convinces the teacher to try a new template. In the "effective" example, the coach asks questions, listens closely, and paraphrases. The teacher provides more details and reflects further. A partnership develops.

Describing the Partnership Carefully

Some terms promote connectivity in the coaching partnership. Others don't. Savvy coaches avoid terms like *coachee*—as in, "The coach meets with the

---

FIGURE 6.2
Questions That Help Coaches Learn More

Ineffective

Teacher: My students won't write up their science labs if I assign them as homework.

Coach: Have you tried using a template that requires students to just fill in the details of the experiment rather than writing everything from scratch?

Teacher: Well, I've used a template that provides the categories of a lab report.

Coach: Let me show you an example of what I mean. See, it gives the text with blanks for providing the methods and findings without asking students to write complete sentences. It helps students who hate to write.

Teacher: I guess I could try it.

Effective

Teacher: My students won't write up their science labs if I assign them as homework.

Coach: Tell me more about that, please.

Teacher: Well, I have a digital lab report form on our course management system, but only about half of the students have internet access at home.

Coach: So half of the students cannot use the template at home. Do the other half use it?

Teacher: Mostly.

Coach: It sounds as though you're concerned about the half without access to the template then, is that right?

Teacher: Yes.

Coach: Tell me what they do.

Teacher: Well, they're supposed to use the hard copy template, but that's more work for them.

Coach: So what happens?

Teacher: Most just don't do it.

Coach: If I understand correctly, the students with access to the digital template do the lab report and those without don't. Did I get that correct?

Teacher: That seems like such a simplification. And it occurs to me that those who don't have digital access at home are also students who live in our poorest neighborhoods, often kids who have moved around a lot. They may have other reasons for not doing their homework that I'm missing.

Coach: Should we partner to learn more?

coachee"—that imply something is being *done to* teachers by coaches. They also avoid using *coach* as a verb to describe what coaches do—as in, "He coached the teacher in how to ask deeper questions" or "That teacher was coached on the new math program"—because it puts teachers in a passive position in relation to coaches.

Communication for Acceptance

When teachers feel that their coach partners accept them, they can be open about what they're experiencing, thinking, and feeling. After all, engaging in problem solving requires that a person share a problem—and that requires a certain level of vulnerability. Coaches' communication skills can enable teachers to feel accepted and, therefore, to become more engaged in the problem-solving process.

Asking Open, Honest Questions

Questioning is essential for effective coaching. However, the nature of the questions makes a difference. Some questions feel intrusive, leading, or like an attack, whereas others are more focused on tuning in and learning more. Parker Palmer's (2004) concept of the open, honest question is helpful in this regard. Coaches will ask an open, honest question because they really want to hear teachers' responses. Open, honest questions are not questions about which the coach has already decided the answer, nor are they questions for which the coach imagines only one acceptable response. When coaches ask such questions, they want to hear teachers' answers and are poised to accept whatever answer the teachers give. Figure 6.3 provides examples of open, honest questions.

One kind of question that a less effective coach might ask really isn't a question. For instance, a coach may ask, "Did you ever think about attending a workshop on cognitively guided instruction in math?" This isn't really a question but is, instead, a suggestion about a workshop that may be helpful. Or, "Do you think those students are bored in class?" Again, this is not so much a question as a statement of the coach's opinion disguised as a question. Savvy educational coaches avoid questions such as these because instead of conveying a coach's acceptance of teachers' thinking, they convey the coach's ideas that the teacher should accept.

FIGURE 6.3

Examples of Open, Honest Questions

Can you describe that further?

What is that like in your classroom?

What do you notice?

What can you tell me about that student?

What concerns you about that?

Could you tell more?

What have you tried?

How would you like this to be different?

Responding Appropriately

How coaches respond to teachers' ideas, descriptions, and questions may or may not convey acceptance. The biggest error that coaches can make is responding to teachers' concerns or problems by providing solutions. In addition to encouraging teacher passivity in problem solving, providing solutions is also a poor communication strategy. It suggests that teachers' problems, concerns, and interests can be quickly addressed—and that teachers could easily solve their problems if they were as knowledgeable as coaches. Here's an important caveat for coaches: *Never think for teachers what they can think for themselves.*

In addition, coaches' responses that convey acceptance are devoid of judgment. They indicate neither acceptance nor rejection of what teacher partners say. For many coaches, this is one of the most difficult parts of the job. As experienced, skillful teachers, coaches have strong theoretical foundations and have decided for themselves what they believe and don't believe, as well as which practices work well and which ones don't. Now, most coaches would never intentionally communicate that they are judging a teacher negatively, but that message is sometimes communicated nonetheless, through body language, tone of voice, or choice of words.

Savvy coaches practice communicating in ways that show acceptance, through a genuine tone of voice, a calm demeanor, and neutral words. However, the best way to communicate acceptance is to have a truly accepting state of mind. Judging but trying not to convey judgment is a lot of work and not always successful. Turning off a judging mind is also a lot of work, but the rewards are worth the effort.

Communication for Trustworthiness

Trustworthy educational coaches take good care of the partnership. They value the relationship and attempt to maintain it. They recognize that teachers can choose whether to engage in coaching or not. Even if teachers are unwisely forced to meet with coaches, it's up to teachers to decide to make it a genuine partnership. Here are some communication strategies that coaches can use to communicate trustworthiness.

Asking Permission

Asking permission is a way to show care for the partnership and remind teachers of their power in the conversation. Coaches might ask permission to move forward, make a suggestion, redirect the coaching conversation, or share something with someone outside the partnership. In each case, coaches need to be genuine in checking in with their teacher partners and willing to accept whatever answer they get. Figure 6.4 provides examples of questions that coaches might use to ask permission of their teacher partners.

FIGURE 6.4
Questions to Ask Permission

Would you mind if I shared an idea that keeps coming to mind?

Could we continue this conversation next time we meet?

I'd like to share a concern that I have. Would you mind?

May I ask a question that may seem off topic but that may be helpful?

Is it OK if I bring some resources to our next meeting?

Would you care to partner to solve that problem?

I'd like to ask [a colleague] about her approach. Would that be OK with you?

May I share that idea with others who might be interested?

Ensuring Confidentiality

For teachers to fully engage in problem solving, they must know that anything they say will be treated confidentially. Therefore, coaches should not share the content or nature of coaching partnerships with anyone in a manner that will identify teacher partners or be used to evaluate teachers. This is one of the most important aspects of coaching, and yet it is violated all the time. The challenge of maintaining confidentiality sometimes arises when coaches work with principals who fail to understand the need for confidentiality; more on that in Chapter 8. However, the challenge also arises when coaches fail to understand the parameters of confidentiality. Confidentiality requires

- That coaches share their notes only with participants in the coaching conversation.

- That coaches do not discuss individual teachers' progress with principals or other supervisors.

- That although coaches might share the overall progress of a school's teachers with others, they cannot share a particular teacher's progress.

- That coaches refrain from sharing individual teachers' successes as well as their struggles because even when a coach praises a teacher to someone else, the coach is still triangulating information. The teacher under discussion may become concerned that *anything* from the coaching partnership is being shared.

Coaches may inadvertently betray confidentiality when asked a question by a principal, teacher, or parent of a student at a moment when their guard is down. For instance, a coach may be chatting with her principal about her own goals, and the principal may say, "I suppose [a particular teacher] prevents you from feeling 100 percent successful." Thinking on the spot is always a challenge, and wise coaches master a few statements that will help them avoid responding with information they do not intend to share. "Let me think about that," "I'm not sure," and "Hmm, I haven't looked at it that way" are some statements I find helpful because they do not commit to agreement or sharing information. Sometimes, silence is best, or a half-smile and a shrug.

Obstacles to Effective Coaching Communication

Coaches need to be aware of some common obstacles to effective coaching communication, including distractions, coach anxiety, urgency to solve a problem, and manipulative language.

Distractions

Coaching is a skillful task that requires focus and engagement. Effective coaching communication is difficult when distractions are present, such as a student waiting to talk to the teacher, a noisy space where other educators are working, or another task taking the attention of participants in a coaching conversation. Part of taking care of the coaching partnership is ensuring that conversations occur in quiet, private spaces and with the full attention of all partners. Wise coaches will reschedule a meeting rather than try to talk about the important work of teaching when distractions are present.

Coach Anxiety

Educational coaches, especially those new to the position, may find themselves worried that they are not doing their job well. Such anxiety might lead to poor communication. For example, coaches might rush to give advice because they feel ineffective without doing so. Or they might forget part of the problem-solving cycle in order to appear to move along more quickly. Or they might disrupt their attentiveness by telling jokes or relating personal stories in an attempt to be liked. Coaches are wise to recognize their own worries and learn to quell their anxiety through centering, focus, and developing confidence in the coaching problem-solving process.

Urgency to Solve a Problem

Urgency is similar to anxiety in that it can skew coaches' language toward giving advice or rushing the process. It most often arises when a coach feels that a problem facing a teacher must be solved immediately.

When coaches feel such urgency, their first tactic should be to reflect on whether the situation is indeed urgent. In most cases, it won't be. Typically, coaches feel urgency when teachers struggle with an issue of importance or one about which the coach feels strongly. These are valuable topics for coaching, but coaches can address them using the coaching cycle, repeatedly reminding themselves that the cycle will be productive and that this important matter will, indeed, be addressed. In those rare instances where the problem is indeed urgent, such as a case of child endangerment, savvy coaches will step out of their coaching role and indicate that the teacher needs to act on the situation immediately, usually drawing on the assistance of the principal.

Manipulative Language

Coaching communication that includes certain terms may leave teachers feeling that the coach is attempting to manipulate them, whether that's the coach's intention or not—for example, "Why don't you . . . ?" or "Did it ever occur to you that . . . ?" Wise coaches will watch for these words and phrases and use them cautiously, if at all. A few of the most common are found in Figure 6.5.

Language feels manipulative when it is perceived as being used to invisibly sway a person's thinking, actions, or perceptions. Coaches don't need to be cyphers—they don't have to pretend to have no opinions or preferences—but they also should avoid trying to impose their thoughts and feelings on

---

FIGURE 6.5
Terms That May Be Perceived as Manipulative

Caution: Are you trying to manipulate the situation when you use these terms?

Why don't you . . .

If only you would . . .

We [when you mean *you*] . . .

Let's [when you mean *you*] . . .

Did you think about . . .

I wish . . .

I wonder . . .

Could it be that . . .

Did it ever occur to you that . . .

Is it possible that . . .

others. Savvy coaches only occasionally offer their perspectives and then do so explicitly.

For instance, in a conversation about language development, a coach might want to remind kindergarten teachers of the value of play by saying, "Do you think we are forgetting the value of play in this conversation?" This statement is manipulative because it is an opinion phrased as a question and because it uses *we* when the coach means *you*. (Clearly, the coach himself is not forgetting the value of play—which is why he is bringing it up!) A more authentic way to raise the topic might be to say, "I keep recalling the research about play as a supportive way for language to develop in young children. Would you mind if we considered that for a few minutes?"

Supportive Responses to Sour Statements

A colleague of mine has pointed out that, at a certain point in one's professional life, most of the work is *people work*. In other words, after a certain amount of experience, most professionals have mastered the knowledge and skills of their work well enough to no longer find them challenging, even though in most fields there is always room to grow. However, the work that involves people— mainly communication and collaboration—never ceases to present challenges.

Sometimes this people work for coaches includes unexpected statements that teachers may make. Figure 6.6 provides a few statements that coaches might encounter—such as, "I don't need your help!"—and suggests some possible ways to respond. Of course, coaches need to find responses that work well for them. In general, such responses should enable coaches to learn more from the teachers making the statements and be made calmly in an even tone, without defensiveness.

Conclusion

Coaches' partnerships are strengthened by effective communication that connects, accepts, and develops trust. Communication that directs teachers in what to do is only helpful to a limited extent; problem-solving conversations usually lead to greater and more long-lasting effects. Coaches should be watchful for situations in which they feel anxious, feel a sense of urgency, or feel compelled to sway their partners into thinking or feeling a certain way because the communication used in such situations is often nonproductive.

FIGURE 6.6
Challenging Statements—And Possible Responses

TEACHER SAYS	COACH MIGHT SAY
You are wasting my time.	• I want this time to be worthwhile for you. What might happen during this conversation for it to be of value?
Just tell me what to do.	• I would never presume to know what you should do. But I'd be glad to partner with you to think about the options available to you and what might be getting in the way.
Why don't you just give me the answers?	• I know that you are an experienced professional. If answers were easy, you would have thought of them already. I hope we can partner to ponder this situation and consider possible answers together.
I don't need your help.	• I hear you. Can you tell me a bit about your class and your successes? • A partnership might be about learning together or developing new ideas; it doesn't necessarily mean you couldn't do it without me.
I've been teaching for 25 years. I don't need a coach.	• Tell me about your 25 years, please. • As a coach, I want to partner with you to focus on enhancing your students' success. We can all use a partner in this challenging work! • [And perhaps add] Our partnership might focus on a particular student, an area of the curriculum you're working on, or an interest you'd like to pursue.
Why don't you just come to my classroom and teach a group of students?	• Tell me more about those students, please. • [And perhaps] When you think about the learning you want those students to do and the teaching you want to do, what gets in the way? • [And, if pushed] My schedule doesn't allow me to come regularly to work with a group of students, but I'd be glad to problem solve with you about them.

Chapter 6 Vignette Revisited

Andre Brooks decided to take a chance and video record some coaching conversations to see if he could identify why his conversations seemed ineffective. He turned to two teachers with whom he had collaborated for years even before he was in a coaching role and who trusted him enough that they gave him permission to record the conversations. Andre wanted to get the advice of another coach colleague, Latisha, and the two teachers graciously agreed to allow Andre to share the video recordings with her. Andre sent Latisha four recordings—two conversations with each teacher—to view before they met, and Latisha gave Andre the "homework" of writing out each question he asked and the teachers' responses.

Andre recognized from this task that his teacher partners, even these two who were professional friends, grew increasingly quiet as the conversation proceeded. When Andre and Latisha met, they looked at the questions Andre was asking. With Latisha's help, Andre recognized that he often asked questions and made statements that hinted at judgment, such as, "Did you ever think that the problem was with your classroom setup?" and "I wonder what would make those boys so bored." Andre then sat in on some of Latisha's coaching conversations, with the teachers' agreement, of course, and heard Latisha using very different language, such as, "What have you tried?" "What do you notice is occurring?" and "Say some more about that, please." Andre spent time practicing his language in mock coaching conversations with Latisha and even refined his questioning skills in his conversations at home with his husband. Then he returned to his own coaching conversations with a commitment to asking more open, accepting, and productive questions. It has been a slow process, but Andre is finding increased success in truly engaging his teacher partners in the conversation.

7

Problem Solving with Teams

> How do coaching partnerships with teams differ from those with individuals?

> How can a coach connect, accept, and be trustworthy with teams?

> How does a coach help several teachers determine what's getting in the way of their success?

....

Chapter 7 Vignette

In his third year as an instructional coach at Pleasant Valley Middle School, Nick Kaminsky has decided to move from individual coaching partnerships to collaborating with teams. Teams in his school consist of the core subject teachers in each house—with four houses per grade levels 6, 7, and 8—and the special educators who work with each house. Nick decides to start small and asks one team from each grade level if he can attend their meetings, a request that is received heartily. As the meetings progress, Nick feels frustrated that he is sitting in on meetings to plan field trips, order supplemental reading materials, review the calendar of integrated units for the house, and discuss other activities that are not what he sees as the purpose of a professional learning community. After several weeks, Nick offers to lead the meetings of one team and facilitate teachers' professional development in the process. The team members agree but feel confused about the shape the meetings might take. Nick assures them that the meetings will be just like his coaching sessions with individuals.

He begins the first meeting by asking The Question: When you think about the learning you want students in this house to do, what gets in the way? The team members produce a list of 18 items, but when Nick asks them where they'd like to start, one teacher speaks for the group and says that they definitely have to focus on the homework policy. Nick proceeds to start a coaching conversation on that topic but finds some members looking distracted and others quiet. Only the person who chose that topic has much to say about it, with others murmuring assent. Nick leaves the meeting regretting he ever stepped up to the plate.

Teachers in many schools collaborate on professional learning teams or communities. The problem-solving cycle is as useful to teams of teachers as it is to individuals. This chapter will focus specifically on that topic—coaches' collaboration with teams.

Individuals Versus Teams

I'm often asked whether educational coaching is more effective with teams or individuals, and my answer is that it depends on the school. In some schools, the teams, whether they're called professional learning teams (PLTs) or professional learning communities (PLCs), are well organized and meet regularly. Those conditions optimize coaching, but another condition must also exist: Different teams must meet at different times. If all teams meet at the same time, it is impossible for a coach to partner with more than one.

In addition, coaching with professional learning teams is effective only in those schools where the "L" in PLT is emphasized—that is, where teams meet for the purpose of *learning* together. In some schools, teacher teams meet to plan together, to develop curriculum, to pass on administrative information, and for myriad reasons other than learning together. All these activities can be valuable, although the groups probably shouldn't be called professional *learning* teams or communities, and, without a focus on learning, coaches' involvement is likely to be unappreciated or turn into something other than coaching.

In schools where PLTs are about professional learning at least part of the time, where PLTs are scheduled so that educational coaches can meet with several or all of them, and where teams are well organized and meet regularly, coaches' work with teams can be highly effective. In these schools, coaching a group rather than individuals also makes good use of coaches' time. However, where these conditions are lacking, coaches are wiser to work with individuals. And, in some schools, coaches find optimal conditions for working with some teams and with some individuals, which can be a fine approach.

Using the Problem-Solving Cycle with Teams

The problem-solving cycle works well with teams as well as individuals. However, the characteristics of working with several people at a time require that coaches develop some skills specifically for use with teams.

Choosing a Topic

The first step in the problem-solving cycle of coaching is determining what gets in the way of teachers' success. The coach should start by asking The Question: When you think about the learning you want your students to do and the teaching you want to do, what gets in the way? When working with an individual teacher, typically at this point the teacher identifies a string of conditions and then selects one to focus on during the coaching cycle.

A similar process occurs when working with a group. After asking The Question, the coach will need to guide team members to select one problem to focus on. The coach should invite each member of the team to share one thing that is getting in the way, then go around the group a second time, with each person sharing a second item, and so forth until all group members' concerns have been listed. When working with an individual, coaches typically list the teacher's concerns on a piece of paper, an electronic tablet, or a laptop. However, when working with a team, savvy coaches will use a chart tablet or whiteboard, which allows all participants to see one another's ideas.

When all obstacles to success are listed, the coach should invite participants to identify their priority item—that is, the item of most concern or that they find most interesting. As members share their items, the coach checks them off on the chart or board. This reduces the list of potential topics to the number of people in the group or to even fewer items if some participants choose the same topic. For instance, if a team of four teachers identified 15 things that are getting in their way, and then each teacher selects one item as a priority, the list becomes those four items. If, in that same group of four, two teachers identified the same item as a priority, then the list is winnowed to three.

Once the list of concerns has been narrowed, the coach likely wants to sit back and let the team members determine which of those "finalists" will become the topic for consideration. I have engaged in this activity with many teams and find that teams usually come to a decision quite quickly. True, some members may not get their first choice, but all seem to understand that the decision is a group decision. I do remind participants that I will save the original list and that we can start with it when we begin the next problem-solving cycle.

Learning Together

When coaches and individual teachers work together, two people are bringing information and ideas to the table. Moreover, as I pointed out in Chapter 4, the partners might do some learning together if they find they do not have enough information to understand a problem at the start. In the case of professional learning teams, the group has the advantage of learning with several others. This is a true asset. For instance, if team members are trying to understand the obstacles to success for a group of students, say, English language learners, there are multiple sets of eyes and ears to gather and share information, such as student data, classroom observations, and parent interviews.

In my experience, the challenge that comes with teams learning together is that sometimes some team members make themselves the experts. More experienced teachers may decide they know the solution to a problem before it has been fully understood and believe that telling others how to solve it is all that is needed. For instance, I once observed a group that identified students' lack of interest in reading as a problem to consider. One teacher proceeded to explain her system of rewards for students who read a certain amount each evening. Beyond the fact that rewarding reading with prizes is ineffective, this teacher's urge to jump in with solutions led to the kind of problem solving that plagues education today: trial-and-error approaches in which the teacher makes a quick decision to try something before taking the time to understand the problem, set a goal, consider multiple possible solutions, and decide how to evaluate whether the approach was successful.

The coach's task when someone jumps in with a quick solution is to gently slow the group down. A coach might say something such as, "I hear that you have an idea of what could be done, Leslie, and I don't want to lose it as a possibility, so I am writing it in my notes. However, I'd like to spend some time talking about the problem to increase our understanding of it. We can come back to solutions a bit further along."

Deciding and Trying

Just as the number of participants is an advantage in the Understanding phase of the problem-solving cycle, so, too, it helps in the Deciding and Trying phases. When teachers in a professional learning team have understood a problem and have set a goal for solving it, the brainstormed possibilities for how to meet the goal are richer when several people contribute ideas. And when several people collaborate in deciding what to try, they can actually try more than one thing at a time. For instance, if a team of four science teachers is considering methods for helping students learn academic vocabulary, the team members might identify 10 options on a brainstormed list and then select four to try, one for each teacher. This can accelerate learning because each teacher benefits not just from her own experience but from the experience of three colleagues as well.

When team members decide to try different teaching strategies, arrange their schedules or classrooms differently, or engage in some other action on which they will report back to the group, coaches play a valuable role in helping them develop criteria to use to evaluate each endeavor. Too often, teachers set out to try something in their classrooms and report back to their colleagues such general impressions as, "The students loved it" or "It was a lot of work." Coaches can help teachers develop a plan for evaluating whether the team met its goal. As discussed in Chapter 3, strategies for evaluating progress to the goal might include the use of formal data, such as exam scores, or checklists, rubrics, and other formative assessment data. Coaches can then assist team members in sharing their findings and making decisions about approaches they might want to adopt in all their classrooms.

CAT Skills for Teams

If the saying is true that two heads are better than one, then the three, four, or five heads that make up a professional learning team are really great! The challenge in learning together as a team is that people come with more than heads or brains. They come with feelings, experiences, wishes, beliefs, and myriad other qualities that make humans interesting but can make collaboration challenging. This is where coaches' CAT qualities of connecting, accepting, and being trustworthy are essential.

Connect

Coaches and professional learning team members may have different ideas about the purpose of the team and the role of the coach. To connect well with teams, coaches need to discuss these matters with team members. It helps if a school principal has already been clear about the team's purpose—and whether that purpose is professional learning.

When teams focus entirely on professional learning, the coach can play a valuable role in partnering for problem solving to help team members optimize their success. However, when teams focus on a variety of topics, one of which is professional learning, coaches may want to negotiate how often the team will partner with the coach and at what times the team will attend to other matters. For instance, if a professional learning team meets weekly to discuss grade-level or department initiatives as well as to engage in problem solving for enhanced success, then the coach may meet with the team every other week, to engage in professional learning and problem solving, with the intervening weeks reserved for other matters.

Teams more than individuals may want to pursue an interest or do more than just solve a problem, particularly if members of the team differ in their teaching backgrounds and experiences and have unique problems that they would rather work on individually. For instance, a team may decide to learn about a cross-curricular topic, such as disciplinary literacy, or they may decide to address a common student quality, such as autism or intellectual giftedness. To guide teachers in pursuing a topic or an initiative, coaches can use the same cycle for problem solving, starting with a variation of The Question: "When you think about [topic], what questions arise?" or "When you think about implementing [an initiative], what might get in the way?" Another approach coaches can use to support team members' interests is to facilitate a book study group. See Chapter 9 for more on that task.

Connecting with everyone on a team means that all team members need to engage with the team's efforts. Sometimes, the most successful teachers have the lowest level of engagement with their teams because they are already experiencing a high degree of effectiveness in their classrooms. It's especially important in these situations for coaches to optimize the learning that occurs among team members. When all team members learn, all see the value of collaborating. To connect well with all team members and optimize the connections that team members have with one another, coaches should

- Be explicit about the problem-solving cycle and how the team will implement it, so everyone understands how the team will work together.

- Provide plenty of wait time when asking questions, especially out of consideration for shyer team members who may need a moment to build courage before speaking.

- Use prompts such as "Anyone else?" or "Any other thoughts?" to encourage multiple views.

- Just as you might differentiate for student strengths by permitting multiple ways to learn and communicate, offer teacher teams options for using technology, representing ideas visually, knitting or standing during the meeting, and other accommodations for varied styles.

A common practice among teams is delineating team norms at the start. I once had an insight about this process when I was on a new committee at church. We were meeting in a room that was used for religious education on Sundays and as we were listing norms for the committee, I glanced at a chart on the wall and saw that the 5th graders had drawn up an almost identical list! These norms are so obvious, I thought, even 5th graders know them.

Now, although children are often in the process of learning how to work on teams and benefit from discussing norms of teamwork, teachers know the norms. So, to me, creating norms for a professional learning team seems unnecessary. My other insight is that the teacher who might choose to violate a norm, such as failing to take turns or to listen respectfully, will do so whether team members have developed a list of norms or not. The problem is not that this adult does not know what is expected!

Coaches are wise to talk to an individual outside of the team meeting if they believe that person's behaviors are disrupting the connectivity that other members wish to experience. The challenge is for the coach to tune in to the person whose behavior seems disruptive. Asking a variation of The Question, such as, "When you think about how you and others might collaborate on the team, what's getting in the way?" can be a good place to start. Form this question carefully, though, so it doesn't sound like a reprimand.

Although team members surely understand the norms for working together, they may want to develop routines for working together—for example, how often the team will meet, for how long, where, who will facilitate, the process for setting the agenda, and the method of taking notes.

Accept

An obstacle to the success of many professional learning teams is that some members do not feel accepted. This could arise for many reasons, with most of them having to do with differences—from differences in teaching background, to differences in years of experience, to differences in philosophy, to differences in race or gender. For instance, the only woman on a team of physical education teachers may experience a feeling of separation, as might a teacher with 30 years' experience on a team with all younger teachers or a teacher who implements inquiry projects while his colleagues focus on textbook-based learning.

Coaches who want all team members to feel accepted must demonstrate that acceptance themselves. They do so first by checking their attitudes and making sure that they do, indeed, perceive all members of the team as valuable and deserving of respect. Pretending acceptance likely will not ring true. Coaches demonstrate their acceptance by their actions, using the same neutral tone of voice with all and monitoring body language so as not to appear turned toward or away from any given team member.

Coaches sometimes stumble by inviting team members to share a preference or an opinion and then responding to the first or loudest voice. For instance, a coach may ask team members how they would like to share information about what they learned on a topic, and an influential team member may say, "Let's create a digital document where we can post comments." If the coach says, "OK, great idea," the coach has privileged that person's ideas. A better approach would be to say, "I hear one idea, which is to create a digital document. Let's consider that and think of other options as well. What other ideas do you have?"

Occasionally, a professional learning team includes a person who really doesn't want the team to do its work. Typically, that person is anxious about sharing in a team or about how they appear to their colleagues, and they attempt to halt the team's work through intimidating language or behaviors. Examples of intimidating behavior include physically turning away from the group, appearing eager to leave by wearing a coat and jangling one's car keys, and loudly sighing or mumbling under one's breath. As for intimidating language, its purpose isn't to communicate but to show one's superiority through the use of unfamiliar terms and obscure references.

Intimidation is a challenge for coaches who want to show acceptance but who don't want such behavior to disrupt the work of the team. Something to keep in mind is that one can accept a person without caring for the person's words or actions, challenging as that is to put into practice. I once saw something on Facebook that suggested that a person with dementia may be difficult because they are having a problem, not because they *are* a problem, and I think that applies to a person showing intimidating behavior as well. Coaches who keep this in mind will have an easier time accepting the person despite the behavior.

Savvy coaches gently tune in further to the intimidating person. The goal is to acknowledge such people and give them a chance to express a need or concern without allowing them to disrupt the work of the team. Coaches can do this by directing attention to the person in a low-key, nonthreatening manner, using a neutral tone of voice, and asking a question such as, "What's up?" or "Can I help you with something?" In this way, coaches provide an opening for the person to explain their perspectives without labeling what might be going on or putting the person too much on the spot. In the case of a person using intentionally abstract or obtuse language, coaches might just ask the person for more information, in order to clarify what the person is referring to and perhaps even to learn something from that person. In this way, coaches show acceptance and give the other person a chance to explain, although often the person won't wish to do so, given that the goal is to stop what is happening, not engage further.

A helpful practice is to check in occasionally with team members between meetings. When coaches ask each member individually how the teamwork is going, coaches may learn more about team members' needs and preferences. I ask two questions: *How is the team helping you to better serve your students?* and *Are you comfortable with your participation in the team?* A person who is very anxious about being part of the team may not feel comfortable opening up, even in a one-to-one situation, but it's worth a try.

If a person struggling to participate in a group continues to display intimidating behavior, it may be best for the coach to work with the person individually. A coach can honestly tell the group something such as, "I have noticed that Marlene's experience and interest is different from the rest of the group, so I suggest I work with her one-to-one. I will continue to meet with the rest of the team together." Of course, to avoid ratcheting up her level of anxiety, it is important to talk to Marlene first, so she is not taken aback at the announcement.

Develop Trust

Being trustworthy is the same whether coaches are working with individuals or teams: Create a safe space for coaching, never presume to speak or decide for your partners, and always, always, honor confidentiality.

A pitfall for some coaches working with teams is that they engage in discussion about the team with individual members outside the team meetings. It may be productive to talk about the content of the team's work outside of a team meeting—for example, if a teacher agreed to gather more data before the next team meeting and then approached the coach individually for advice on how to do so. Conversation outside the team's meetings is also appropriate if the coach wants to understand individuals' own experiences on the team for the purpose of improving coaching. However, it likely will reduce coaches' trustworthiness if they talk about the people on the team with individual team members. By doing so, coaches risk being perceived as playing favorites or gossiping. Savvy coaches remind team members at the start that discussions about the team's collaboration are best held in the team setting.

Conclusion

Coach partnerships with teams of teachers provide opportunities for rich learning as team members listen and learn from and with one another. Coaches benefit from a few extra skills to make team problem solving effective and ensure that everyone engages well. As in all coaching endeavors, connecting, accepting, and being trustworthy are essential characteristics for team coaching success.

Chapter 7 Vignette Revisited

After Nick Kaminsky's less-than-successful start in facilitating a professional learning team in his school, he spent a good deal of time reflecting. He had had many effective coaching conversations with individuals and pondered what was different with the team. After talking it through with a coach colleague, Nick realized that an added task when coaching teams was, for lack of a better term, crowd management. He recognized that in that last meeting, he had listened to the first person who spoke up rather than finding a way for everyone to participate in choosing a topic, and he had failed to include everyone in the conversation that ensued. Nick sat in on a team coaching conversation that his colleague was leading (with the teachers' permission, of course) and learned the process that team used to select a topic. When he returned to his own team, he asked them to back up and revisit their topic selection, a process that led to choosing a topic of interest to all members. Nick has continued monitoring how he responds to group members who are quiet, as well as to those who are vocal, and to find a way to connect with all of them.

8

What Gets in *Your* Way?

> How come a few teachers don't want to work with me?

> What do I do when my principal doesn't understand coaching?

> How do I find time for coaching conversations?

> How do I avoid burnout as a coach?

Chapter 8 Vignette

When Nancy Thao began her job as a math coach at Rowling Elementary School, she was sure that she would never fill her days. That concern quickly passed, however, as her calendar became increasingly full. Now, in February of her first year as a coach, Nancy is exhausted and behind. She doesn't have a spare minute in her day, what with committee meetings, school leadership meetings, Response to Intervention (RTI) coordination meetings, student evaluations, preparation for staff in-service days, presentations at the PTO meetings, and stepping in for the assistant principal when she is gone. Moreover, Nancy doesn't know whether she is making a difference in her school. She has gotten to know many of the teachers, and some come to see her to vent. In addition, they do seem to respect her viewpoint when she speaks up at meetings. But, Nancy wonders, is that enough? And if it *is* enough, can she maintain this pace for the rest of the year and for years to come?

Coaching usually involves rewarding partnerships with teachers who are engaged and committed to collaboration. However, like any job, there are bumps in the road. Coaches occasionally encounter someone who isn't interested in a partnership. Coaches occasionally work with principals or other administrators who don't understand effective coaching. Occasionally, an entire school has a challenging environment. And finding enough time is always a challenge! With the demands placed on coaches, there is always a chance that coaches will become unwell or burn out. This chapter will help coaches approach all of these matters to overcome obstacles to their success.

People Who Don't Want to Partner

Sometimes when coaches are unsuccessful in connecting with a colleague, they label the teacher resistant, difficult, or uncaring. I suggest an easier way to look at the situation is merely to conclude that the teacher does not want to partner with the coach at this time. This description avoids negative labels and avoids presuming to know what the teacher is feeling or perceiving, always a good approach when people surprise you.

Although I discourage guessing, I suggest that coaches tune in to teachers who may not want to partner to learn more about the teacher, the teacher's classroom, and the teacher's thinking about coaching. Figure 8.1 provides some suggestions for how to respond when teachers don't seem to want to collaborate with a coach.

In general, those who hesitate to partner with a coach fall into one of three categories: They don't understand coaching, they don't feel comfortable with the coach, or they feel anxious talking with others about their teaching. Remember, it is not wise to presume that one of these three situations is the case, but coaches who tune in further and learn that one of them is may find the ideas below helpful.

Teachers Who Don't Understand Coaching

Coaching is still misunderstood by some educators. For instance, they may think it is a supervisory activity, only for "bad" teachers, or about telling

---

FIGURE 8.1
Responding to Teachers Who Don't Want to Partner

Teacher: I don't need a coach.

Coach: I understand. I wouldn't presume that you need to work with me. But I'd love to listen and learn about your class. At minimum, I'll be enlightened, and maybe we will find a place for partnership. Tell me about some of your successes, please.

Coach: When you think about the learning you want your students to do and the teaching you want to do, what gets in the way?

Teacher: Nothing.

Coach: Sounds like you are experiencing a good deal of success. I'd love to hear about it.

Coach: When you think about the learning you want your students to do and the teaching you want to do, what gets in the way?

Teacher: You!

Coach: Really? Tell me how.

Teacher: I've been teaching a lot longer than you have. There's nothing you can tell me.

Coach: You're right! That's why my goal is to partner. I would never presume to think I know more than you, but sometimes it is good to have another set of eyes or ears. Tell me about your classroom, please.

---

teachers what to do. Here are some ways that coaches can help teachers understand coaching:

- Develop a concise statement about what you do, and use it often to refer to your work. For instance, you might say, "As a coach, I partner with teachers to enhance student success" or "Coaches collaborate with teachers to solve problems and build on their strengths." Think about the understanding you want teachers to have and then identify key words and phrases that you want to use. Then use them over and over again so that you and your colleagues own them.

- Introduce yourself at the start of every school year, at a faculty meeting, if possible. Use this opportunity to remind colleagues what you are all about and what coaching is all about. You might start with your concise statement about coaching but then expand on it to convey your CAT characteristics—how you Connect, Accept, and develop Trust. See Figure 8.2 for an example of what you might say, but make it your own.

- Share a handout with an overview of coaching when you introduce yourself to teachers with whom you haven't worked. (See Figure 4.1 for a sample handout.)

- Explain coaching on your own professional web page.

- When you arrange appointments to meet one-to-one with a teacher, ask if they have any questions about coaching.

Teachers Who Don't Feel Comfortable with the Coach

Sometimes teachers don't want to work with a particular coach. Coaches are wise to try to tune in to what may be on the teacher's mind, but typically when a person doesn't care for another person, they don't want to share that information. Therefore, a coach may have to rely on a hunch that that may be the case. Some clues are that teachers in this position often are vague about their reasoning or may have been successful in partnering with others but not with the coach. Coaches who suspect that a teacher doesn't want to work with them in particular may want to find opportunities to get to know the teacher and let the teacher get to know them, in noncoaching situations. For instance, a coach may seek out opportunities to visit with the teacher at lunch, serve on a committee with the teacher, or socialize with the teacher at a holiday gathering or special interest activity for staff members.

I discourage coaches from giving up on any teacher. Check in periodically with teachers who are hesitant about collaborating and see if they might like to

---

FIGURE 8.2
Introducing Yourself as a Coach

Hello, everyone! For those of you whom I haven't yet met, my name is _____, and I am the educational coach for our school. In that capacity, I will partner with you to solve problems and enhance strengths. I will start the year meeting with each of you one-to-one to learn about you and your classroom and consider how we might collaborate. I'd also like to partner with your PLTs if your team would like that. I consider it an honor to be a coach in this school and, as always, I will honor our conversations with respect and confidentiality.

have a visit. And consider inviting those teachers to be part of a professional learning team or book study group, during which they can participate quietly without feeling as on the spot as in a one-to-one situation.

Teachers Who Are Anxious

If you observe closely, you will see that anxiety is behind much of our worst behavior as human beings. People snap at a store clerk who miscalculates the tab because they are worried they will be shortchanged; parents of injured children speak harshly in the doctor's office because they fear that their child won't get the proper medical care; drivers lay on their horn and make rude gestures because they're on edge after another car has almost caused a serious accident.

And so it is with teachers. Anxious teachers will not always be on their best behavior, and sometimes it is difficult to see the anxiety because they have masked it so well with what appears to be criticism, confidence, or rudeness. Actually, coaches do not have to identify anxiety; they just need to be aware that it likely is present if a teacher is acting in a less-than-stellar way toward them. And many teachers are particularly anxious about invitations to talk about their teaching if that work is not going well.

The best response from coaches, then, is the CAT response. First, connect with the teacher in some way, even if it's outside a coaching partnership. Then, accept whatever the teacher is presenting. This is sometimes difficult if the teacher's anxiety leads to harsh words or rude behaviors. However, savvy coaches accept that at that moment, that is the best the teacher can do. If they can stay in the present moment rather than get caught up in their own worries, coaches likely will be able to calmly interact with the teacher when opportunities arise. (See Figure 6.6 for a chart of possible responses to challenging statements from teachers.) Finally, coaches should maintain trustworthiness by avoiding any temptation to criticize the teacher to others or gossip about her.

Beyond coaches' CAT qualities, some strategies can help when interacting with anxious teachers:

- Always start by listening. For instance, ask for more information, how a coaching conversation could be useful, or what the other person would like you to know.

- Attempt not to be defensive. Remind yourself that the situation probably is not about you personally.

- Stay centered and in the present moment so *you* don't become anxious.

- Focus on less anxiety-producing matters if possible. For instance, if a teacher seems anxious when describing students who are struggling, ask about students who are experiencing success.

- If appropriate, acknowledge anxiety. For instance, if a team is preparing to look at standardized test scores, say something such as, "It's always a little nerve-wracking to open these documents, isn't it?"

- Check your own language to ensure that you're not inadvertently raising the anxiety level by seeming to manipulate the situation. (See Chapter 6 for more on this topic.)

- Slow your breathing and breathe from your diaphragm. (You know this is happening if your tummy extends when you breathe in and retracts when you breathe out.) Research on mirror neurons tells us that when one person calms, another one nearby may do the same.

Administrators Who Don't Understand

As a former school administrator, I understand firsthand how full a principal's day is and how much information a principal must know. It is easy to see why an administrator, especially a school principal, might miss the details of a coach's job. However, it is important to a coach's success that administrators understand the model of coaching being implemented, the general duties of the position, and how administrators can support coaches. Many times, administrators who have not taken the time to learn about coaching seem to assume that coaches are quasi-principals who mildly supervise teachers and then behave in a friendly way to get teachers to do what coaches want. This understanding of coaching is counterproductive to effective coaching and can lead to problems for coaches.

When coaches work with administrators who have inaccurate views of coaching, they have two jobs. In the short run, they need to find ways to succeed in that situation. In the long run, they need to help administrators learn about coaching. In regard to the first challenge, there are several steps coaches can take to avoid being pulled into a flawed perception of coaching.

- Be sure to explain yourself and your role to the staff so teachers can hear from you how you envision your work.

- Talk to the principal about the importance of confidentiality and ask her assistance in reminding you of its importance if you are ever heard to slip. In this manner, you make the principal aware that coaching is a confidential task; it may help to prevent the principal from asking you details of your partnerships with teachers.

- If a principal attempts to engage you in conversation about teachers, ask for the principal's help in understanding the necessity that you maintain the confidentiality of your coaching conversations. If the principal pressures you to talk and you don't know what to say, tell the principal you'd like to think over your response and ask to talk again another day. That gives you time to compose an explanation about confidentiality without having to respond while on the spot.

- If a principal tells you to work with certain teachers who are not successful, ask the principal to talk to those teachers and ask them to contact you, rather than you contacting them. In that way, the principal's supervision will not be triangulated, with you in the middle between the principal and teacher. In addition, you will not have to explain to the teachers why you are approaching them, and the teachers will be able to control what they do or don't tell you, which is appropriate for a professional partnership. From a supervisory standpoint, this approach is also savvy because it places the responsibility for professional growth on the teacher; the principal working with such a teacher can then ask about the coaching partnership as part of the supervisory relationship with that teacher.

In regard to coaches' second task, that of helping principals to grow in their understanding of coaching, savvy coaches will engage in an ongoing effort to expand principals' views. Here are some ways to do so:

- Discuss a book, such as this one, and tell your principal it really got you thinking; ask to share a few highlights. (Resist the urge to give the principal a copy and expect her to read it; principals usually have a stack of items that require immediate attention on their desk and a stack twice as high of materials they wish they had time to read!)

- Provide a one-page overview of coaching and ask the principal for a few minutes at a staff meeting to share it with everyone in the school. In the process of informing everyone, you'll inform the principal. (See Figure 4.1 for a one-page coaching overview.)

- Create a professional web page about your work, and ask the principal to look it over before you share it with the staff.

As with all work of coaches, remembering to use one's CAT qualities is valuable. Connect positively with principals, accept that they're doing their best, and behave in a trustworthy manner, especially by avoiding manipulative language or behavior.

Schools Without Focus on Collaboration or Teacher Learning Time

Occasionally coaches find themselves working in schools that lack optimal conditions for successful coaching partnerships. Optimal conditions for coaching include

- A knowledgeable and an engaged principal.

- A spirit of *learnership*—that is, leadership for learning—among administrators and teacher leaders.

- Open commitment to professional learning among all teachers and staff members.

- Trust among faculty and staff.

- Opportunities for collaboration beyond coaching partnerships.

- A value placed on teacher reflection and decision making.

The opposite kind of school is one in which teachers are tightly controlled from the top down, curricula are scripted, teachers work as individuals without professional collaboration, professional development takes the form of telling people how to follow the rules, administrators are distant and regulatory, and anxiety pervades. Now, most schools have several positive conditions and an occasional negative; no place is perfect. However, occasionally a coach is asked to work in a place that simply has few positives; often, the hope is that the coach will fix the place, which, of course, is outside the realm of coaching.

Coaches in the rare situation of being in a school bereft of conditions supportive of coaching have some short-term and long-term matters to consider. In the short term, they are wise to lower their expectations. For instance, instead of hoping for productive problem-solving cycles with eight professional learning teams, a coach might hope to find one group of teachers that wishes to give it a try. And instead of partnering for deep coaching conversations with most of the teachers in the school, the coach might settle for friendly conversations with a bit of substance.

In the long term, coaches in such schools will want to consider their options. They might decide to stay at the school and do what they can, leave the school for another coaching position, or determine what's within their power to change. Turning around a struggling school is beyond the scope of this book, but I do have some advice for coaches who go the latter route: (1) Don't go it alone—identify teachers, other staff members, and parents of students who will work with you; (2) be transparent about your efforts so you don't seem subversive; and (3) recognize that this work is beyond your duties as a coach and that you're exceeding your job description, if you have one; make sure you want to take the risk of engaging in such an endeavor.

Working in a school that does not reflect qualities essential for effective coaching is difficult, to say the least. Coaches in such situations are wise to adjust their expectations and proceed with caution.

Time

When the topic of time comes up in a workshop that I am leading, coaches eagerly raise their pens or excitedly place their hands on their keyboards, ready to take note of the wisdom I'm about to impart. Inevitably they are disappointed because neither I nor anyone else has the solution to the problem of time. Virtually everyone is short on time, and that's certainly true of coaches.

So what's a coach to do? This section provides suggestions to help coaches manage their time well and perhaps eke out a few extra minutes in the day.

Finding Time for Coaching Conversations

Educational coaches need time to do their work. That seems obvious, and yet in all too many schools, coaches do not have enough time for coaching because they have myriad duties that have nothing to do with coaching. Now, some coaches are assigned to more than one role, as when teachers are assigned to coaching duties 50 percent of the time and to providing instruction to students, such as Title I services or intervention, the other 50 percent. In those cases, the challenge becomes one of preserving one's allocated coaching time; it is so easy to have that time eaten away by obligations from one's other roles. Keeping a coaching log (see Figure 8.3) or doing an occasional time study

FIGURE 8.3
Sample Coaching Log

Coaching Log

For the Week of ___*March 7*___ to ___*March 11*___

Date	Activity	People Included	Notes
March 7	*Demonstration lesson*	*A. Brower, D. Fleming*	*Demonstrated mini-lesson on revision of writing*
	Team meeting	*Grade 7, House A*	*Developed goal related to grading student projects*
	Coaching conversation	*M. Colson*	*Continuing to develop unit using UDL principles*
March 8	*Team meeting*	*Grade 8, House C*	*Shared evidence of success with integrated unit*
	Coaching conversation	*R. Voelker*	*Identified support for English language learners as topic for next cycle*
	Coaching conversation	*L. Hanson*	*Reviewed data collected about students failing in math*

(see the section "Finding More Time") can help keep the appropriate balance between roles.

An inadequate coach-to-teacher ratio presents another challenge. For instance, some coaches work in large schools where they are expected to work with 40, 60, or even 100 teachers. Other coaches are assigned to several smaller schools, leading to a cumulative load of more than 50 teachers, plus drive time between schools. These are unreasonable demands on coaches. When coaches have too many teachers to work with, generally defined as more than 25 teachers assigned to a full-time coach, they are wise to ask their school leadership team to identify a pool of teachers with whom the coaches might work.

The pool of teachers might be developed by looking at staffing patterns, course content, student placements, or student data. School leaders might use that information to determine places where teaching is especially challenging, such as

- If English language learners are placed in one classroom per grade level at an elementary school or in certain sections of courses in a high school, those classes would be particularly challenging to teach.

- Courses with demanding reading requirements, such as literature or history classes, might be especially challenging to teach.

- Classrooms with fewer adults working in them might be more challenging to teach in, when compared with classrooms with several aides or resource teachers.

- Student data may indicate that in a subject such as math, students begin to struggle at a certain grade or in certain courses—say, when they reach 7th grade or when they take algebra—and therefore those courses may be especially challenging to teach.

When such a pool is formed, principals are wise to explain this action to the entire staff by saying something like, "The School Improvement Team has examined a number of factors, including student placements and staffing patterns, and we have determined that the three houses that have English language learners placed in them are especially challenging for the teachers. We know that all of you would enjoy working with the coach, but we believe it will be best for her to start the year focused on collaborating with teachers in those houses where the challenges are even greater than elsewhere." The goal in making such an announcement is to clarify the thinking of the leadership team, emphasizing the reasons that the pool was formed and making sure that no one gets the impression that teachers in that pool are less capable or successful than other teachers in the school.

Scheduling Coaching Conversations

I encourage educational coaches to spend at least 50 percent of their coaching time in coaching conversations, helping teachers solve problems and enhance their success. And I encourage coaches to ask teachers for a minimum of 30 minutes of their time for a one-to-one coaching conference and at least 45 minutes for a team meeting. This is not an easy task, given how busy teachers are.

Of course, coaches might meet with teachers before and after school and during planning time, although they should never presume that teachers will want to meet during those times. Wise coaches always work with teachers to find the best times to meet.

Teachers might find additional time to meet with coaches by thinking creatively about how they could collaborate to share students. For instance, in an elementary school where older students engage in "buddy reading" with younger students by reading together for 30 minutes every week, the teachers involved might share supervisory duties, with the teacher of the older students overseeing the buddies one week and the teacher of the younger students doing so the next week. The teacher who is not supervising could meet with the coach. Or, in a high school where two or more teachers teach sections of the same course, one teacher might supervise two classes as students do online research or watch a video while the other teacher meets with the coach. These arrangements don't always work out, but sometimes they do if teachers are creative and are committed to meeting with the coach.

An ideal way for coaches to meet with teams of teachers is to bring a few substitute teachers into the school and have them rotate to different classrooms. For instance, four subs might cover for four English teachers during the first hour of the day, then for four math teachers, then for four science teachers, and so on. During the period when a teacher has a sub in his classroom, he and the rest of his team can meet with the coach. Such an arrangement might make it possible for a coach in a small high school to meet with most of the professional learning teams in one day. True, some schools cannot afford substitute teachers or cannot find enough subs on a given day, but again, it's worth a try, particularly if the day is midweek and not in flu season. Keep in mind, too, that in some school districts, money allocated through Title I or the IDEA grant might be used to pay substitute teachers for this purpose.

Finding More Time

To better manage your time, you might want to do a time study. Here's how. Carry a clipboard or an electronic tablet with you for an entire week, and record everything you do—everything. Complete a chart that itemizes the time, location, activity, and others present for all of your actions, recording even when you make a phone call or go to the restroom. Then analyze the data you collected to see patterns: Are you spending a lot of time with certain people? Are you engaged in many tasks that are unrelated to your coaching duties? Are you overlooking a department, grade level, or team? How often are you answering the phone or replying to e-mails? How much time do you spend in meetings? Use the findings to consider changes you want to make.

Coaches may benefit from sharing what they learn from a time study with their supervisors. The information could be enlightening to supervisors who are unclear about how coaches spend their time. In addition, the identification of problem areas might lead to beneficial changes in assigned duties. For instance, a time study may reveal that a coach is spending too much time organizing testing materials or supervising study halls, and this insight could prompt a principal to reassign those duties.

When seeking to create more time for coaching, you might try any of the following ideas (with thanks to Sandholtz, Derr, Carlson, & Buckner, 2002, for the seeds of the first three ideas):

- "Chunk" certain activities by doing them all at once. For instance, answer phone messages only once a day, after lunch, or respond to e-mail messages at identified times, rather than being distracted by them throughout the day. It may be helpful to leave a voice message on your phone or an automatically generated e-mail response alerting others if you plan to respond at a certain time of the day.

- "Outsource" tasks that could be done by others. For instance, 6th graders could keep the book room organized with a little training from the coach, or a high school student looking for IT experience could build your website.

- Use technology to save minutes. For instance, place an article on your website rather than copying it for all the teachers who want it, or share digital copies of coaching notes with your teacher partners, rather than trekking to the printer or copy machine for paper copies. In regard to coaching notes, if you want them to be digital, enter them into a laptop or tablet during the conversation; retyping notes after the conversation is a waste of time. In the not-too-distant past, it seemed that people were annoyed when a partner took notes on a computer, but these days everyone seems used to it.

- Reduce interruptions and distractions so you can make the best use of your time. For instance, schedule coaching conversations only when you and your partner are available for 30 uninterrupted minutes, and hold those conversations in a closed-door space where others will not interrupt. Or, when you need to accomplish a task—say, preparation for a demonstration lesson—use a "Do Not Disturb" sign on your office door, like the ones that can be placed on hotel room doors when one wants to sleep in.

- Think cost-benefit. In other words, ask yourself, will the benefit of this activity be worth the cost in time? For instance, serving on the school's social committee may not have the same benefit as serving on the math committee if you're a math specialist. Then again, sometimes it's good to chip in and help out just for fun.

- Don't give up on parent volunteers. There used to be a day when many parents, most of them mothers, worked at home and were more available to volunteer in schools. These days, fewer parents can come during the school day, but some may be willing to give a couple of hours each week in the evening after their children are in bed. Perhaps a parent could update the database of instructional materials when new items are ordered or jazz up your PowerPoint presentation for a workshop.

Your Well-Being

Sometimes the biggest obstacle to coaches' success comes from within, when they are not feeling well mentally, emotionally, or physically. Of course, all people need to take care of themselves and, given the demands placed on educators, this is true of all of us in the profession. However, the visibility of educational coaches' work and the challenges of being in a role that is sometimes misunderstood mean that coaches are especially vulnerable to illness and stress. Here are some reminders about how coaches can maintain their well-being:

- **Note your accomplishments.** It seems to be human nature to focus on our mistakes rather than successes, but educational coaches seem to struggle with this in particular, perhaps because they often leave their own classrooms, where they were highly successful, for new roles in which they have much to learn. So create a *Hurrah!* file on your phone, tablet, or laptop and record one success every day.

- **Develop a support system.** Of course it's good to have friends, spouses, and family members who listen and cheer us on, but the best support system for the challenges of coaching is other coaches. Find a network or create one of your own if none exists in your area. (You can find some tips for how to do so in Chapter 5.)

- **Keep learning.** Continue to solve problems and develop your own understanding and strengths through reading books and articles and attending workshops. Consider extending your research beyond the field of education; my coaching practice has been informed a great deal from the reading I do in the fields of management, psychology, linguistics, and philosophy.

- **Find ways to relieve stress.** Stick to healthy stress-relievers, such as movement, nature, music, and pets, with an occasional chocolate bar or glass of wine for good measure.

- **Develop practices for being centered.** Engage in meditation, yoga, prayer, or any other practice that grounds you in the present moment and calms your breathing.

- **Don't own all the problems.** As the song says, let it go. Or as the prayer says, accept the things you cannot change.

- **Have hope.** Believe in yourself and your colleagues, trusting that you're all working to improve yourselves to help the students you serve.

Conclusion

Just as educational coaches recognize that things get in the way of teachers' success, so do obstacles such as misunderstanding administrators, teachers who don't engage, time constraints, school conditions, and stress get in the way of coaches' success. Coaches' own problem solving can move them beyond these limitations to be even more effective in creating partnerships with teachers.

Chapter 8 Vignette Revisited

One day, Nancy Thao "dumped" on her principal, breaking down in tears. Nancy confessed that she was exhausted, but at the same time she questioned whether her many activities were making a difference in the school. After listening, the principal showed Nancy how to do a time study and invited Nancy to bring her findings back for a discussion a few weeks later. Nancy was eager to look more closely at her time use and engaged in the time study the following week.

When she analyzed the data, she was surprised. Sixty-two percent of her time had been spent in meetings of one kind or another. She had only one coaching conversation all week. She spent a lot of time—almost 10 percent of her week—in the hallway chatting informally with teachers, parents, and students. And her efforts focused almost entirely on the planning and implementation of RTI.

These data revealed the need for some changes, which she and her principal worked on when they met. Over the following months, Nancy made a concerted effort to schedule coaching-related duties first, especially coaching conversations. She withdrew from one committee and invited a teacher to co-chair the RTI committee with her. She and the principal discussed turning over more of the RTI decision making to teachers, and they reduced Nancy's responsibilities for all-staff professional development workshops. In May, Nancy did another time study and found it reflected much better use of her time. More important, she found she was purposeful in her work and went home most days feeling she had accomplished something.

9

Additional Tasks for Coaches

> What should I do when I am not having coaching conversations?

> Should coaches lead workshops for teachers?

> How can I make demonstration lessons effective?

> What do coaches do if they are asked to oversee implementation of new initiatives or programs?

> What is my role in Response to Intervention (RTI)?

> Is there a way to connect my work with students to my work with teachers?

Chapter 9 Vignette

Shreya Anand is a successful curriculum coach at North High School. She has made positive connections with most teachers and has many coaching partnerships that have enhanced teachers' success. She loves most aspects of her job but feels frustrated by the request that she lead a two-hour teacher professional development session once a month throughout the school year. It takes many hours for Shreya to plan each session, and she often perceives that teachers are a little resentful of the time that preparation takes from her work with them, as well as the time that the workshops take away from the teachers. The sessions feel like a disruption of her coaching work and leave her questioning their effectiveness. She wishes there were a way to eliminate the professional development sessions altogether or, if that is not possible, to find a better way to connect them to her coaching practice.

Although I encourage educational coaches to engage in problem-solving conversations at least 50 percent of the time, I understand that coaches will necessarily have other duties to attend to. In this chapter, I will highlight ways to support teacher success through coaches' demonstration lessons, professional development workshops, study groups, implementation of programs and initiatives, and support of RTI. I'll also describe a method for linking coaching to work with students and discuss classroom observations.

Demonstration Lessons

Demonstration lessons can be helpful to teachers as they seek to be more successful, but demonstration lessons often fail to be effective. Some of the reasons for the failure of demonstration lessons are

- They focus too much on what teachers *do* rather than on teachers' thinking, especially their decision making.
- Coaches' demonstrations fail to connect with what is currently being studied in a particular classroom.
- Coaches' lack of understanding about classroom procedures or students' needs leads to unproductive distractions when the coach fails to honor classroom routines or interacts with a student inappropriately.
- Teachers leave the classroom during the lesson.
- The lesson occurs in isolation from a coaching partnership.

The processes described in this section likely will enable coaches and teachers to avoid potential downfalls and make demonstration lessons valuable.

Build Demonstrations from Coaching Conversations

Well-intentioned coaches sometimes announce their availability to do demonstration lessons on a particular topic and then wait for teachers to request one. I recall making this blunder early in my experience as a reading specialist, when I made available a sign-up sheet for teachers who wanted me to demonstrate think-aloud procedures for constructing meaning from text. Only one teacher expressed interest, and I believe it was a "pity sign-up," meaning she felt sorry for me when she saw the empty sign-up sheet.

A better approach is to build demonstration lessons out of the coaching conversation. With this approach, coaches only do demonstration lessons when their teacher partners express an interest or need for which a demonstration would be effective. For instance, if a team of middle school social studies teachers is exploring ways to use movement in their classrooms, particularly to help English language learners, a coach might offer to demonstrate a practice he found helpful in his own classroom. The teachers are already interested in the topic, so they're likely to be interested in the demonstration.

Have a Pre-Demonstration Conference

Coaches are much more likely to be successful in providing demonstration lessons if they first have a conference with classroom teachers to understand what's going on in their classrooms and how the demonstration fits into the instructional program. When coaches and teachers pre-plan demonstration lessons together, coaches learn the answers to these important questions:

- What content is the teacher currently teaching? With this information in hand, coaches are able to select a topic and related materials that will enhance the unit being implemented at that time.

- What unique needs do students have? Coaches will be better prepared for a successful lesson if they learn in advance about students' special needs, such as the need for assisted learning devices, and students' unique qualities, such as a student who is emergently bilingual.

- What routines or rituals will students expect? Lessons go more smoothly when coaches know what the students expect, such as routines for how students move into and out of small-group discussions or the schedule for some students to leave the classroom for individual musical instrument lessons.

Another important topic for the pre-demonstration lesson conference is clarifying the role of the classroom teacher. I have done demonstration lessons in which teachers felt responsible for behavior management and therefore disrupted the lesson with verbal corrections of individual students. I have also done demonstration lessons where I wished the teacher would circulate and listen in on students' conversations when they were working in pairs, something I had failed to communicate to the teacher beforehand. Clarifying the teacher's role in advance can further the effectiveness of the lesson. A sample pre-conference form is provided in Figure 9.1.

FIGURE 9.1
Demonstration Lesson Planning Sheet

Date of demonstration lesson:

Location of demonstration lesson:

Objectives of lesson:

Background information:

    Students:

    Curriculum:

    Class rituals/rules:

Role of classroom teacher during lesson:

Date and time for follow-up discussion with teacher(s):

Post-lesson reflections of coach:

Some coaches provide teachers with an observation tool to use during demonstration lessons. This one-page questionnaire prompts teachers to reflect on certain aspects of the lesson as they observe. When coaches ask teachers to complete such a form, it focuses teachers' attention during the lesson, increasing the chance that teachers will stay in the classroom and will watch closely, and it provides a helpful resource for a post-demonstration conference. Figure 9.2 provides a sample.

Have a Post-Demonstration Conference

Coaches and teachers are busy people. Sometimes when they manage to find time for a pre-demonstration conference and demonstration lesson, they feel they have done enough. However, a post-demonstration conversation is also in order. Here, teachers and coaches can

- Discuss what the coach did to enhance student learning, considering what students did, how they interacted, and what they may have produced during the lesson.

- Discuss anything in the lesson that inhibited student learning, noting points where the students appeared confused, distracted, or uninterested.

FIGURE 9.2
Observation Questionnaire
(For teachers' use during demonstration lessons)

---

1. What strategies do you see being demonstrated? What details do you notice about how each strategy is being implemented (for instance, what is the coach saying or doing)?

2. What signs of student success do you notice? What conditions are facilitating this success?

3. What signs of student frustration do you notice? What conditions are contributing to this frustration?

4. What adaptations would you make to this lesson?

- Consider modifications to the lesson that teachers might try, including the use of different instructional materials, an alteration in the lesson sequence, the expansion of parts of the lesson for further explanation or exploration, or anything else that would make the lesson more effective for the group or groups of students with whom the teacher works.

- Discuss the coach's thinking, decision making, and behaviors during the lesson to further teachers' understanding of the *why* as well as the *how* of the demonstration.

- Reflect on how the demonstration might increase teachers' success by discussing the teachers' goals, identified in the coaching conversation, that led to the demonstration lesson in the first place.

A demonstration lesson without a follow-up conversation is like a meal served without seasoning. Sure, it's palatable, but the experience is so much more valuable when it's properly completed. Figure 9.3 provides a sample post-demonstration conference form that will help coaches and teachers properly flavor their collaboration.

Whole-Group Professional Development

Coaches are frequently asked to provide whole-group professional development activities, usually in the form of workshops, to the faculty and staff members at the schools in which they work. Now, coaching has often developed in response to the perceived ineffectiveness of such activities; for generations, whole-group workshops have been the primary professional development opportunity offered to teachers, and for generations, teachers have complained that these workshops are a waste of time. A well-known study conducted by Beverly Showers and Bruce Joyce (2002) found that educators could enhance the effect of workshops by providing follow-up opportunities for practice—and, yes, coaching. This study, as well as research on adult learning, led educators to advocate for educational coaching.

However, whole-group workshops are not entirely useless. The study by Showers and Joyce found that there was indeed an effect, although somewhat small, of workshops on teachers' understanding and practices. Workshops often introduce a new idea or practice by creating awareness and enhancing

---

FIGURE 9.3
Post-Demonstration Follow-Up Conversation

Participants in follow-up conversation: Date:

Topic of demonstration lesson: Classroom:

Points to make about coaches' decisions made during the lesson:

Student behaviors and responses:

Possible modifications and extensions:

Reflections on the usefulness of the lesson in helping teacher(s) meet goal:

---

understanding. Coaches wishing to optimize teacher success might follow two key steps for enhancing the workshops they facilitate: Get to know what's on teachers' minds, and connect workshops to coaching conversations.

Learn About Teachers' Knowledge and Concerns in Advance

One of the flaws of whole-group professional development workshops is that they often begin and end where the presenter or planners think they should. A better approach is for coaches to understand teachers' knowledge and concerns about the topic as the starting point and develop goals for the workshop based on teacher input. For some coaches, their coaching conversations will have provided information about these matters, which is great because that means the topic is already on teachers' minds. In other situations, coaches may want to develop a questionnaire for teachers to complete before planning the session.

Follow Up with Coaching Conversations

Connecting a whole-group workshop to teachers' own classrooms, interests, and challenges is essential for optimizing its effectiveness. Savvy coaches modify their question at the start of a follow-up conversation, asking something like, "When you think about implementing [the ideas/practices from the workshop] in your classroom, what seems like it will get in the way?" The ensuing problem-solving session will enhance teachers' abilities to bring the workshop to life in their own work.

Study Groups

Teacher study groups can be a wonderful way for teachers to learn together. Sometimes, professional learning teams or professional learning communities conduct study group activities, but often they occur independent of other small-group teacher teams as voluntary activities. The most common forms of study groups are inquiry groups, in which teachers investigate a topic together, such as spelling instruction or formative assessment, and book study groups, in which teachers read and discuss a professional book.

The coaches' role in study groups varies. Coaches sometimes join a group as a participant. In that role, coaches obviously can learn a lot about the topic; in addition, they can get to know their colleagues and their colleagues' interests and concerns. But coaches can play two other roles: Sometimes they facilitate a group at the request of the teachers who participate, and sometimes they initiate a study group as an offering to the teachers in a school or district. Let's look at how coaches might optimize these roles.

Facilitating Study Groups

Coaches' CAT qualities of connecting, accepting, and being trustworthy are useful in facilitating study groups. Helping others in the group use similar skills is also valuable. Here are some tips:

- Plan an initial activity for group members to get to know one another. Even among teachers who have worked together a long time, there are always new ways to connect. A starter I like for those who already feel well acquainted is, "Tell us one thing we wouldn't know about you if you didn't tell us." This invitation often leads to shared stories about early life experiences, travel, hobbies, and the occasional funny secret.

- When leading an inquiry-focused study group, help the group clarify exactly what they are investigating. For instance, teachers in a study group devoted to emergent bilingual students (sometimes called English language learners) might inquire into students' first languages, instructional strategies, collaboration with parents, or many other aspects of the topic. It might be fruitful for group members to look at a topic from many angles, but often it is more productive for group members to focus their attention on just one.

- When the study group focuses on a book all the members have read, ask open-ended questions that will help group members take the conversation in the direction they choose. See Figure 9.4 for examples.

Initiating Study Groups

Study groups can be a way for coaches to go beyond problem-solving conversations to support teachers' interests. However, those one-to-one or team conversations often provide the information coaches use to plan study groups. For instance, a coach may frequently hear that what gets in the way of teachers' success is teachers' lack of innovative ways for students to engage in discussions

---

FIGURE 9.4
Open-Ended Questions for Book Study Groups

What strikes you as most relevant in this book for your situation?

How has this book made you think in a new way?

Is there anything that surprised you in this book?

Is there anything puzzling in this book?

Do you know anything about the author that influenced your reading of the book?

Did this book remind you of anything else?

If a colleague asked you whether you recommend this book, what would you say? Why?

When you think about applying the ideas in this book, what might get in the way?

or their own lack of insights into the home cultures of immigrant students. When coaches hear a similar concern from several teachers, they may want to initiate a study group. Here are some tips for doing so:

- If the group will read a book, select two to four possible titles and do a book talk for each at a faculty meeting to get teachers interested and give them an idea of the kind of book they may read. Then invite teachers to vote on the title to be read. An added benefit will be that for those who don't join the book study group, you will have made them aware of some valuable professional resources.

- When offering a study group on a particular topic, briefly describe that topic when announcing the study group. Don't assume that everyone shares the same understanding of a topic. For instance, topics such as *integrating the arts, disciplinary literacy,* or *engaging all learners* might have different meanings for different people.

- Be clear about what you envision for the study group. Will there be "homework"? Will members read one book or draw on several resources? How often do you envision the group meeting, or will you let group members decide? Where will you meet?

- Consider inviting all staff members—not just teachers—to participate. Teaching assistants, guidance counselors, principals, and others may find the group of interest.

A personal note about study groups—and food. People often assume that food is essential for a successful meeting. As someone who prioritizes making good choices in what I eat and drink but who often struggles to do so, I sometimes find it torture to sit around a meeting table where a big plate of brownies is inches from my nose! I know that those with certain health conditions, such as diabetes, struggle in those situations as well. Sometimes the solution is to provide a variety of snacks, but in my experience, it's so easy to look past the bowl of apples and focus on the chocolate chip cookies. I encourage study group participants to agree on whether there will be snacks and on what kind they prefer. Perhaps in one group, participants will all delight in gooey, chewy treats, and if so, I say go for it! But participants in another group may decide to go a different route or may recognize that they can have a rich conversation without any additional calories.

Coaching for Initiatives

Administrators sometimes create coaching positions to promote implementation of new programs, instructional materials, practices, standards, or some other major initiative. Some coaches may believe that this requires a different approach from the one presented in this book, but that is not the case. When coaching for initiatives, coaches still use their CAT qualities, but the focus is a bit more specific.

Connect

When coaching for initiatives, coaches' starting question in the conversation likely will be, "When you think about implementing [the initiative], what seems like it will get in the way?" This focuses teachers' attention on the new program, materials, or curriculum, but it also leaves plenty of room to address any potential problems that may impede their success with that initiative.

Accept

When something new is introduced in a school, some teachers will eagerly jump in, some will hold back, and some will even push back against it. All these positions are fine as starting points—as long as coaches start where the teacher is. For instance, a teacher who is eager to make the initiative his own may partner with a coach to think about how to find time in his schedule, whereas a teacher who is confused about what is being asked of her may partner with the coach to learn more.

Coaches who work with teachers who resist an initiative may find good results in asking these teachers to consider the best possible outcome of what appears to the teacher to be a less-than-ideal situation. For instance, if a teacher fails to see the benefit of implementing writing workshop in her classroom, a coach might say, "I can tell that this is not your first choice in how to organize your class time. However, given that it is a mandate for all members of the English department, what would be the best possible outcome for students?" A question such as this one acknowledges a teacher's hesitation while inviting consideration of what might occur that could benefit students.

When considering these "resistant" teachers, it may be helpful for coaches to think about times when they resisted someone else's idea, such as a spouse's interest in buying a boat, a doctor's recommended treatment, or a daughter's desire for a tattoo. They may realize they resisted for very good reasons: Spouses say no to big purchases when they want to be responsible with the household budget, patients ask for another line of treatment when they believe the doctor's recommendation is not right for them, and parents tell their children they cannot have tattoos because they don't want their children marking their bodies for life before they are old enough to make that decision carefully.

Teachers who resist a school initiative likely have reasons that make perfect sense to them and reflect admirable qualities. For instance, a teacher may believe that a new set of instructional materials will make learning difficult for some students or may find that a new requirement detracts from precious instructional time. When coaches recognize the worth of their own resistances, they may have an easier time seeing the positive forces behind many teachers' hesitance to adopt new initiatives. This insight may help them refocus their conversations with teachers and be gentler in the process of helping teachers move forward with the initiative.

Be Trustworthy

When something new is introduced, school leaders are often eager to monitor its implementation. In such situations, principals may ask educational coaches to report on teachers' progress. Savvy coaches are careful to provide an overview of the implementation but not specifics about any one teacher. For instance, if teachers in an elementary school are implementing a new math curriculum, a math specialist asked about teachers' progress might say, "I find that everyone is moving along. For some, full implementation is occurring. Others are still learning about it, and a few are struggling to begin, but we are working on that. I'd say that schoolwide, we are about two-thirds of the way in fully implementing the curriculum." If pressured to tell the principal who those few strugglers are, the coach might gently say, "I'm wary to mention names because I'd be concerned that those teachers would stop talking to me about their reservations, in which case I couldn't help them. Could you talk to teachers yourself to find out where they are in the process? That way, I can continue to garner the trust of my teaching partners."

Work with Students

Coaches' clients are teachers, so coaches' work with students should only occur when they're providing demonstration lessons for teachers to observe. However, when coaches have split roles, such as serving as coaches 50 percent of the time and working with students the other 50 percent of the time, they might use their work with students to initiate coaching partnerships with teachers.

For example, coaches who are working with students, say, in intervention or in Title I, might invite teachers to meet to talk about those students they both are working with. Then coaches might ask a question such as, "When you think about the learning of this student [in math, reading, or whatever the area of focus], what seems to get in the way?" As the teacher identifies obstacles to the student's success, the coach and teacher might identify one area that they will work on together using the problem-solving cycle. This process can benefit coaches when they're in their instructional role by enhancing their success in supporting the student as a learner, and it can develop a strong coaching partnership as well.

Response to Intervention

Response to Intervention (RTI) is implemented in different ways in various school districts, and educational coaches play varying roles in relation to RTI. In general, coaches participate in RTI by being part of a decision-making team, supporting teachers in enhancing their instruction, or providing interventions themselves.

RTI Decision Making

The RTI process requires assessing and monitoring students and planning increasingly intense levels of intervention. Most school districts have a team that leads the RTI process and, except in the smallest districts where the leadership team serves this purpose, a school-based team that makes decisions about individual students. Educational coaches have much to contribute to both teams, but they're not always present on either team, a fact that puzzles me a great deal. If anyone were to ask me, I'd say coaches should top the list of potential members of any RTI team.

When coaches are part of the RTI leadership team, they need to be aware of two general approaches to RTI: (1) the standard protocol model, which depends on fidelity to an intervention, usually designed by a company and sold to the school or district, and (2) the teacher problem-solving model, which depends on teachers' knowledge and skill in determining students' instructional needs (Fuchs & Fuchs, 2006).

Readers of this book will recognize that teacher problem solving is the basis for much of the coaching work I recommend; it is my preferred approach to RTI as well. I hope that coaches who understand the power of teacher problem solving will feel the same way and use their understanding of problem-solving processes to advocate for those processes among RTI leaders as they develop or revise a district's RTI program. Not every RTI leadership team will adopt the problem-solving approach, of course, but coaches on the team might be able to present the case for it.

Coaches' involvement in decision making about individual students can be powerful as well. As experienced teachers, coaches have insight about students, teaching, and learning. In addition, many coaches have expertise either in a core subject area, such as reading or math, or in assessment and data analysis, any of which will make coaches valuable members of an RTI team. In addition, all experienced coaches likely possess questioning skills they can use to prompt team members to think carefully about the data presented and the interventions being considered.

Support for Teachers in the RTI Process

The problem-solving cycle of coaching is perfect for coaches' support of classroom teachers when they seek greater success with students in the RTI process. Coaches and teachers together can understand students more deeply, set a goal, plan to meet the goal, and then collect evidence to indicate whether the goal has been met. In fact, this *is* the RTI decision-making process used in many districts that implement the teacher decision-making model of RTI. In districts using the standard protocol model, coaches can still support teachers in solving problems related to implementing the prescribed intervention.

Coaches as Interventionists

Many educational coaches provide instruction to students who are receiving Tier 2 or Tier 3 interventions as part of their jobs when they are not coaching.

Given coaches' past successful teaching experience, it is logical for them to provide intervention services, and they are likely to do an excellent job. However, I'm not convinced that providing RTI services is the best use of a coach's time and skills. (Note here that when I say "coaches," I mean people who are assigned coaching duties part time and intervention duties part time. Intervention is not part of a coach's actual coaching duties.)

First, there are practical issues. Intervention work typically occurs on a daily basis, which means coaches must be in a particular place at a particular time every day for intervention. For most coaches, such a commitment leads to a trade-off: More time with students leads to less time with teachers, their coaching clients.

Second, when coaches work with students, they use their expertise to limited effect. For instance, a coach who works with five students over the course of a semester has the net effect of increasing the achievement of five students. A coach who works with 20 teachers over the course of a semester has a net effect of enhancing the achievement of all the students those teachers teach, both presently and in the future; the net effect is the improvement of learning for thousands of students.

Third, when coaches provide interventions for a few students in teachers' classrooms, they do nothing to increase the capacity of those teachers. On the other hand, when coaches partner with teachers to help them plan and implement interventions, they expand teachers' capacity. This is coaching at its best.

Finally, evidence shows that RTI services are most effective when provided by teachers who know the students well (Tissiere & Lieber, 2012). Too often, the students who struggle most in school are forced to work with multiple teachers for core instruction, whereas students who find school easier stay in their own classrooms and work with their familiar teachers. This backward system can be turned around when coaches help classroom teachers provide interventions for those who need them most.

Coaches wishing to optimize their effectiveness will reflect on these matters with their colleagues and supervisors to determine how to best make use of their time and skills. In regard to their role as a coach, providing interventions is often not the best decision.

What? No Observations?

Careful readers will notice that nowhere in this chapter or in the entire book have I discussed observing teachers in their classrooms. This is because I rarely do observations as a coach. There are several reasons for my decision:

- Showers and Joyce (1996) reported findings of their study of peer coaching teams in which they found no effect when a coach observed a teacher and provided feedback.

- For many teachers, being observed feels like supervision, no matter how hard a coach tries to convince them otherwise.

- Observation, by its nature, focuses on the practices of teaching and fails to include consideration of teachers' knowledge, decision making, and perspectives.

- An observation is like a snapshot in that it captures one segment of a day, but it fails to incorporate factors and influences beyond the time of the observation.

- Observing is not a good way to start a partnership. It makes one person, the coach, the knowledgeable other and creates an inherent power differential, however subtle.

I will observe in a classroom if a teacher realizes that a second set of eyes would help her to understand a student. At that point, I'm observing the students, not the teacher. Even then, I first discuss with the teacher whether it would be better for me to teach and for her to observe the students; it could work either way, depending on the situation. And I always first meet with a teacher for a coaching conversation.

Coaches sometimes worry that they won't know what's occurring in a classroom if they do not observe. When I suggest that coaches can listen and learn from teachers about their classrooms, these coaches express doubt that teachers will accurately represent what's occurring in their classrooms. Let's consider such situations: If a teacher misrepresents what's occurring in her classroom and a coach catches her misrepresentation by taking a look for himself, what will happen next? Will the coach point out the teacher's misrepresentation?

Will the coach try to school the teacher in what's really occurring? At best, the coach will have to sell his viewpoint to the teacher. At worst, there will be an argument about differing perceptions. None of this leads to a good coaching partnership.

Coaches worried about getting at *the truth* would be wise to remember that the only good place to start in a coaching partnership is where the teacher is in the present moment. If the teacher is not comfortable talking candidly about what may be occurring in her classroom or if a teacher doesn't have the same perception of his teaching as the coach does, the partnership must begin with whatever the teacher *does* perceive or share. Then a skilled coach can help the teacher move through the problem-solving cycle, learning more in the Understanding phase, thinking carefully in deciding on a goal and an action step, and collecting data about whatever step is taken to make further decisions. In the process, teachers come to trust coaches, and coaches help teachers to reflect, learn, and perceive carefully. Sometimes teachers will tell a coach, "Just come observe me and tell me what to do." Savvy coaches respond with something like, "Let's talk first," and they schedule a coaching conversation. Then, by listening and learning, using process skills to facilitate problem solving, and bringing their CAT qualities to the conversation, they'll encourage a partnership that will be much more likely to enhance teacher success.

Conclusion

Educational coaches perform many tasks, even when their priority is the coaching conversation. All coaching tasks are best done by connecting, accepting, and being trustworthy. In addition, coaches can develop skill in doing effective demonstration lessons, providing meaningful whole-group workshops, leading study groups, supporting the implementation of new initiatives, and providing guidance to the RTI process.

Chapter 9 Vignette Revisited

Shreya Anand shared her frustration with the other coaches in her large school district and found that many of them experienced the same concern—that their whole-group professional development sessions were disruptions of their coaching work. Together, they formed a study group to consider options; as a result, they created a digital site on which they shared resources for alternatives to professional development workshops. They also engaged in extensive reflection about the purposes of coaching and of all-staff workshops and sought areas of overlap.

Shreya took all this back to her school's leadership team, and together they decided that they would continue with the workshops but give Shreya more control over two important factors: content, which she then could develop in response to patterns she saw in coaching conversations, and process, which allowed her to end each session by strategizing with teachers how subsequent coaching conversations could support the learning done in the workshop. Shreya's work now feels more integrated and productive.

10

Conclusion: Trusting the Process, Your Colleagues, Yourself

> How can coaches trust the approach to coaching that they are using?

> What are some ways for leaders to support coaches?

Chapter 10 Vignette

Donna LaBonte is the assistant superintendent of a medium-size school district in the suburbs of a large city. When Donna began the position two years ago, she inherited supervision of the curriculum coaches in each school, but she is only now getting around to examining the coaching program and making decisions about its effectiveness. Two of the curriculum coaches attended a workshop on the problem-solving cycle of coaching and have been enthusiastically telling Donna about the coaching partnerships they have been engaged in and the difference the partnerships are making in teachers'—and coaches'—success. Donna wonders whether she should trust these coaches' reports of improved coaching processes and skills and formally promote the problem-solving cycle in the coaching program.

I have worked with thousands of coaches in diverse settings—rural, urban, and suburban districts; big and small schools; networked in regional organizations;

attending international conferences; clustered around a table in a school library. I consistently encounter smart, caring coaches who work hard to do well. And I consistently encounter coaches who are unsure, confused, or frustrated. This coaching business is demanding and has not always been clearly thought through before implementation. There is strong evidence in surveys of coaches that coaches need more support.

I'm going to use this final chapter to remind coaches of tasks and perspectives that are essential for coaching success. It's a summary of key ideas in the book, but I hope it's also a final hurrah that will inspire coaches and send them back to their desks, whiteboards, and conference rooms with renewed vigor.

Among the recurring concepts in this book has been trust. Let's frame these final reminders around that term.

Trust the Process

The processes I have laid out in this book, particularly the problem-solving cycle, are not ones I latched onto at random. In fact, I tried many other approaches to coaching before recognizing the value of these processes, and I have learned a great deal about why they work. The problem-solving model is consistent with adult learning theory, in the sense that it honors teachers as learners who have strong views about what they want to learn and how they want to learn it. The coaching conversation applies an understanding of how people change by giving teachers a say about what they work on and what they do differently in their classrooms. The overall approach to coaching as a responsive and flexible partnership recognizes schools and faculty teams as complex living systems that are always adapting and organizing themselves. In other words, these processes are grounded in research and theory.

Sometimes coaches worry that their teacher partners are selecting bad topics for problem solving or going in a direction that won't work. I smile and tell them to trust the process. So long as coaches follow the cycle of problem → understanding → goal → action plan → try something new → collect information to decide how it worked, everything will work itself out. The process is effective because it starts with what's important to teachers and then supports teachers in looking closely, moving forward, and solving problems.

To trust the process, wise coaches become experts in steering the process. Key tasks of a process expert include helping teachers to

- Identify what gets in the way.

- Resist the rush to try something by first engaging in a process of understanding the matter thoroughly.

- Pursue answers to questions to further understand the problem.

- Envision what it would be like if the problem were solved and use that response to develop a goal.

- Develop a list of possibilities for how they might meet the goal.

- Select one item from the list to try.

- Develop a plan for implementing the selected activity.

- Develop a plan for evaluating the success of what they try.

- Implement the new activity and collect data according to plan.

- Use evaluative information to determine whether what they tried was effective, should be tweaked, or should be thrown out (in which case, they might try another item from the brainstormed list of possibilities).

This is the problem-solving process. Trust it.

Trust Your Colleagues

I hope I have quelled any worries that coaches or their supervisors have about "letting" teachers start where they are—as though we could do anything else!—and grow from there. When supported by a coach partner who is a process expert, teachers will use the problem-solving cycle to enhance their success. Teachers are good people who care about students and work hard to make a difference. Sure, they're human, and therefore they sometimes become anxious or hesitant, but coaches who are authentic and patient will almost always find excellent partners in teachers.

The partnerships I propose give teachers a chance to be their best because they include the following characteristics:

- Coaches bring qualities of Connectivity, Acceptance, and Trustworthiness to the partnership.

- The coaching conversation is job-embedded, meaning that it's about teachers' own work in their own classrooms.

- Teachers are able to focus on matters that are getting in the way of their success; in other words, the partnership is practical and productive.

- Coaches' priority of listening carefully enables teachers to feel understood and appreciated.

A coach with whom I worked received a great compliment when a teacher said, "I feel so smart after meeting with you!" That is coaching at its finest—trusting the wisdom of teacher partners.

Trust Yourself

Confidence in oneself is demonstrated quietly, in a person's posture, eye contact, and use of language to inquire and describe. Coaches' trust of themselves results from their confidence that they're the right people to do the job. Unfortunately, coaches don't always have that confidence, usually because they haven't received training that makes them sure of their skills, sometimes because they don't know what to look for to determine whether they're successful, and occasionally because their supervisors haven't set them up for success.

Professional Development for Coaches

Educational coaches benefit from ongoing professional development opportunities. This certainly could take the form of workshops but, given what readers know about collaboration, it's best when those opportunities take the form of coaching-the-coach, book study, inquiry groups, and professional learning teams or when workshops are followed by one or more of these activities. Coaches might learn about any of the following topics through their own professional development:

- Adult learning theory

- Organizational change

- Communication strategies

- Working with challenging situations

- Formative assessment
- Group processes

Detecting Successes

We humans are not always the best judges of our own successes. Here are some signs of success that coaches can watch for:

- Coaching conversations include greater reflection.
- Teacher partners dig deeper to understand challenging students or problem situations before they decide to try a solution.
- Teachers turn to coaches as partners rather than as the people with the answers.
- Faculty members convey increased confidence in their problem-solving abilities.
- Professional teams spend more time learning together (rather than focusing on administrative matters, planning, etc.).
- Administrators ask teachers about their increased successes as a result of coaching partnerships.

Feedback from Supervisors

Coaches benefit from specific feedback from supervisors. Here are some things that supervisors might watch and listen for:

- Coaches maintain confidentiality in regard to their partnerships with teachers.
- Coaches' schedules or logs indicate that 50 percent of their coaching time is spent in coaching conversations with individuals or teams.
- Coaches help teachers identify what gets in the way of their success and use the problem-solving cycle to move beyond those obstacles.
- Coaches connect whole-group professional development sessions, intervention work, or work with professional learning teams with their coaching conversations.

- Coaches use the problem-solving cycle when asked to help with the implementation of new initiatives.

- Coaches help teachers and others in the school to understand coaching.

- Coaches demonstrate strong listening skills and prioritize listening when interacting with others.

- Coaches ask questions that help teachers think deeply about students, the curriculum, and effective teaching.

- Coaches possess the qualities of Connectivity, Acceptance, and Trustworthiness.

Supervisors will note some of these successes only by sitting in on coaching conversations. I encourage supervisors to proceed with caution if they wish to do so. Select conversations that include teachers with whom you have a positive relationship, and always ask permission of those teachers. Be explicit with the rest of the faculty and staff that you don't plan to sit in on any conversations other than those one or two. Another approach is to invite coaches to record video of one or two coaching conversations, again with the teachers' permission, making it clear that these recordings are the exceptions and not typical. Then, reflect with coaches what they and you notice from the videos or select one or two goals and view the recordings specifically for evidence of meeting those goals. Such feedback from supervisors can help coaches develop confidence and learn to trust themselves.

Conclusion

If I've done my work as an author, readers of this book will have perspectives, practices, and knowledge about coaching that they can use to help teachers solve problems and achieve greater success. I hope that is so.

As I mentioned in the introduction to this book, I welcome readers' insights and perspectives, so please feel free to send me a message through my website, www.partneringtolearn.com.

Chapter 10 Vignette Revisited

Donna LaBonte has been pondering whether the curriculum coaches in her district would be wise to shift to a problem-solving model.

She has visited with two coaches who have been using that model and sat in on some of their coaching conversations, with teachers' permission, of course. Donna also visited with and observed coaches using other approaches, such as a model based on observing teachers, giving feedback, and helping teachers develop new practices, and a model based on looking at student data and asking teachers to come up with ways to improve those data.

Donna is struck by the differences in the processes, the conversations, and the teachers' reactions. She also has been reading research and familiarizing herself with theories about adult learning, organizational change, and complex systems, and she recognizes that the problem-solving model is consistent with much current thinking in these areas. She realizes that it's time to make a decision. She decides to trust the problem-solving model.

References

Ariely, D. (2009). *Predictably irrational: The hidden forces that shape our decisions*. New York: HarperCollins.

Bengo, P. (2016). Secondary mathematics coaching: The components of effective mathematics coaching and implications. *Teaching and Teacher Education, 60*, 88–96.

Blachowicz, C. L. Z., Buhle, R., Ogle, D., Frost, S., Correa, A., & Kinner, J. D. (2010). Hit the ground running: Ten ideas for preparing and supporting urban literacy coaches. *The Reading Teacher, 63*(5), 348–359.

Burbank, M. D., Kauchak, D., & Bates, A. J. (2010). Book clubs as professional development opportunities for preservice teacher candidates and practicing teachers: An exploratory study. *The New Educator, 6*(1), 46–73.

Calvert, L. (2016). *Moving from compliance to agency: What teachers need to make professional learning work*. Oxford, OH: Learning Forward and NCTAF. Retrieved from https://learningforward.org/docs/default-source/pdf/teacheragencyfinal.pdf

Cave J., LaMaster, C., & White, S. (1998). Staff development: Adult characteristics. Batavia, IL: Fermilab. Retrieved from http://ed.fnal.gov/lincon/staff_adult.html

Center for Public Education. (2005). *Teacher quality and student achievement: Research review*. Washington, DC: Author. Retrieved from http://www.centerforpubliceducation.org/Main-Menu/Staffingstudents/Teacher-quality-and-student-achievement-At-a-glance/Teacher-quality-and-student-achievement-Research-review.html

Chaltain, S. (2009). *American schools: The art of creating a democratic learning community*. Lanham, MD: Rowman & Littlefield.

Chval, K. B., Arbaugh, F., Lannin, J. K., van Garderen, D., Cummings, L., Estapa, A. T., & Huey, M. E. (2010). The transition from experienced teacher to mathematics coach: Establishing a new identity. *The Elementary School Journal, 111*(1), 191–216.

Darling-Hammond, L., Wei, R. C., Andree, A., Richardson, N., & Orphanos, S. (2009). *Professional learning in the learning profession: A status report on teacher development in the United States and abroad*. Oxford, OH: National Staff Development Council.

Davis, B., & Sumara, D. (2006). *Complexity and education: Inquiries into learning, teaching, and research*. Mahwah, NJ: Erlbaum.

Diaz-Maggioli, G. (2004). *Teacher-centered professional development*. Alexandria, VA: ASCD.

Doran, G. T. (1981). There's a S.M.A.R.T. way to write management's goals and objectives. *Management Review, 70*(11), 35–36.

Egawa, K. A. (2009). Good talk about good teaching. *Voices from the Middle, 16*(4), 9–16.

Escamilla, K., & Hopewell, S. (2010). Transitions to biliteracy: Creating positive academic trajectories for emerging bilinguals in the United States. In J. E. Petrovic (Ed.), *International perspectives on bilingual education: Policy, practice, and controversy* (pp. 69–94). Charlotte, NC: Information Age.

Fisher, R., & Shapiro, D. (2006). *Beyond reason: Using emotions as you negotiate.* New York: Penguin.

Fuchs, D., & Fuchs, L. S. (2006). Introduction to Response to Intervention: What, why, and how valid is it? *Reading Research Quarterly, 41*(1), 93–99.

Gallucci, C., Van Lare, M. D., Yoon, I. H., & Boatright, B. (2010). Instructional coaching: Building theory about the role and organizational support for professional learning. *American Educational Research Journal, 47*(4), 919–963.

Goe, L., & Stickler, L. M. (2008). *Teacher quality and student achievement: Making the most of recent research.* Washington, DC: Comprehensive Center for Teacher Quality. Retrieved from http://files.eric.ed.gov/fulltext/ED520769.pdf

Hall, G. E., & Hord, S. M. (2001). *Implementing change: Patterns, principles, and potholes.* Boston: Allyn & Bacon.

Hannum, M. (2015). The toxic effects of communication triangulation. [Blog post]. Retrieved from http://blog.linkageinc.com/blog/systems-thinking-5-the-toxic-effects-of-communication-triangulation/

Hargreaves, A. (1998). The emotional practice of teaching. *Teaching and Teacher Education, 14*(8), 835–854.

Heineke, S. F. (2013). Coaching discourse: Supporting teachers' professional learning. *Elementary School Journal, 113*(3), 409–433.

Hinds, E., Jones, L., Gau, J., Forrester, K., & Biglan, A. (2015). Teacher distress and the role of experiential avoidance. *Psychology in the Schools, 52*(3), 284–297.

Hull, T. H., Balka, D. S., & Miles, R. H. (2009). *A guide to mathematics coaching: Processes for increasing student achievement.* Thousand Oaks, CA: Corwin.

International Literacy Association. (2015). Position statement: The multiple roles of school-based specialized literacy professionals. Newark, DE: Author. Retrieved from https://literacyworldwide.org/docs/default-source/where-we-stand/literacy-professionals-position-statement.pdf

Kabat-Zinn, J. (2012). *Mindfulness for beginners: Reclaiming the present moment—And your life.* Boulder, CO: Sounds True.

Killion, J., Harrison, C., Bryan, C., & Clifton, H. (2012). Coaching matters. In J. Killion, C. Harrison, C. Bryan, & H. Clifton, *Coaching Matters* (pp. 7–12). Oxford, OH: Learning Forward.

Kohn, A. (1999). *Punished by rewards: The trouble with gold stars, incentive plans, A's, praise, and other bribes.* Boston: Houghton-Mifflin.

Lynch, J., & Ferguson, K. (2010). Reflections of elementary school literacy coaches on practices: Roles and perspectives. *Canadian Journal of Education, 33*(1), 199–227.

Marsh, J. A., McCombs, J. S., Lockwood, J. R., Martorell, F., Gershwin, D., Naftel, S., Le, V., Shea, M., Barney, H., & Crego, A. (2008). *Supporting literacy across the sunshine state: A study of Florida middle school reading coaches.* Santa Monica, CA: RAND.

Marsh, J. A., McCombs, J. S., & Martorell, F. (2010). How instructional coaches support data-driven decision making: Policy implementation and effects in Florida middle schools. *Educational Policy, 24*(6), 827–907.

Marzano, R. J., Pickering, D. J., Heflebower, T., Boogren, T. H., & Kanold-McIntyre, J. (2012). *Becoming a reflective teacher.* Bloomington, IN: Marzano Research Lab.

McDonald, S., Keesler, V. A., Kauffman, N. J., & Schneider, B. (2006). Scaling-up exemplary interventions. *Educational Researcher, 35*(3), 15–24.

Newton, C. (n.d.). The five communication styles. [Blog post]. Retrieved from http://www.clairenewton.co.za/my-articles/the-five-communication-styles.html

Palmer, P. J. (2004). *A hidden wholeness: The journey toward an undivided life.* San Francisco: Jossey-Bass.

Palmer, P. J. (2007). *The courage to teach: Exploring the inner landscape of a teacher's life, 10th anniversary edition* (2nd ed.). San Francisco: Jossey-Bass.

Poglinco, S. M., Bach, A. J., Hovde, K., Rosenblum, S., Saunders, M., & Supovitz, J. A. (2003). *The heart of the matter: The coaching model in America's Choice schools.* Philadelphia: Consortium for Policy Research in Education. Retrieved from http://www.cpre.org/sites/default/files/researchreport/814_ac-06.pdf

RAND Corporation. (1977). *Federal programs supporting educational change, Volume VII: Factors affecting implementation and continuation.* Santa Monica, CA: Author.

Richardson, V., & Placier, P. (2001). Teacher change. In V. Richardson (Ed.), *Handbook of research on teaching* (pp. 905–947). Washington, DC: American Educational Research Association.

Sandholtz, K., Derr, B., Carlson, D., & Buckner, K. (2002). *Beyond juggling: Rebalancing your busy life.* San Francisco: Berrett-Koehler.

Scientific American. (n.d.). *The mirror neuron revolution: Explaining what makes humans social.* Retrieved from https://www.scientificamerican.com/article/the-mirror-neuron-revolut/

Senge, P. (2006). *The fifth discipline: The art and practice of the learning organization* (Rev. ed.). New York: Doubleday.

Senge, P., Kleiner, A., Roberts, C., Ross, R., Roth, G., & Smith, B. (1999). *The dance of change: The challenges of sustaining momentum in learning organizations.* New York: Doubleday.

Showers, B., & Joyce, B. (1996). The evolution of peer coaching. *Educational Leadership, 53*(6), 12–16.

Showers, B., & Joyce, B. (2002). *Student achievement through staff development* (3rd ed.). Alexandria, VA: ASCD.

Skaalvik, E. M., & Skaalvik, S. (2011). Teacher job satisfaction and motivation to leave the teaching profession: Relations with school context, feeling of belonging, and emotional exhaustion. *Teaching and Teacher Education, 27*(6), 1029–1038.

Smith, A. (2006). The middle school literacy coach: Considering roles in context. In D. W. Rowe, R. T. Jimenez, D. L. Compton, D. K. Dickinson, Y. Kim, K. M. Leander, & V. J. Risko (Eds.), *56th yearbook of the National Reading Conference* (pp. 53–67). Oak Creek, WI: National Reading Conference.

Stark, M. (2002). *Working with resistance.* Northvale, NJ: Jason Aronson.

Tissiere, M., & Lieber, C. M. (2012, April). *Response to Intervention: What it is and how we do it.* Plenary session presented at the Strategic Interventions for Student Success Conference, Washington, DC.

Toll, C. A. (1996, February). I don't sit on the roof. *Reading Today, 13*(4), 14.

Toll, C. A. (2005). *The literacy coach's survival guide: Essential questions and practical answers.* Newark, DE: International Reading Association.

Toll, C. A. (2007). *Lenses on literacy coaching: Conceptualizations, functions, and outcomes.* Norwood, MA: Christopher-Gordon.

Toll, C. A. (2012). *Learnership: Invest in teachers, focus on learning, and put test scores in perspective.* Thousand Oaks, CA: Corwin.

Toll, C. A. (2014). *The literacy coach's survival guide: Essential questions and practical answers* (2nd ed.). Newark, DE: International Reading Association.

Toll, C. A. (2016). A problem-solving model for literacy coaching practice. *The Reading Teacher, 70*(4), 413–421.

Tolle, E. (2004). *The power of now: A guide to spiritual enlightenment.* Novato, CA: New World Library.

University of Florida Lastinger Center for Learning, Learning Forward, & Public Impact. (2016). *Coaching for impact: Six pillars to create coaching roles that achieve their potential to improve teaching and learning.* Gainesville, FL: University of Florida Lastinger Center; Oxford, OH: Learning Forward; and Chapel Hill, NC: Public Impact. Retrieved from http://www.learningforward.org/coaching-for-impact/

Narrative Bibliography

This narrative bibliography provides additional information and references to supplement ideas presented in the book.

Chapter 1

Definitions of Educational Coaching

Below is a sampling of definitions of coaching from research journals, professional books, and professional organizations.

- "Mathematics coaching . . . can be defined broadly as job-embedded learning for mathematics teachers with someone who can help" (Bengo, 2016, p. 88).

- "A mathematics coach is an individual who is well versed in mathematics content and pedagogy and who works directly with classroom teachers to improve student learning of mathematics" (Hull, Balka, & Miles, 2009, p. 3).

- "Defined broadly, coaching is a form of professional learning within the classroom or school that helps teachers develop and apply new knowledge, make strong plans for instruction and assessment, obtain feedback, refine their practices, and examine results" (University of Florida Lastinger Center for Learning, Learning Forward, & Public Impact, 2016, p. 3).

- "Coaches [are] master teachers who offer onsite and ongoing instructional support for teachers" (Marsh, McCombs, & Martorell, 2010, p. 873).

- "[A literacy coach is] primarily responsible for improving classroom instruction by supporting teacher learning and facilitating literacy program efforts" (International Literacy Association, 2015).

Criticisms of "Sit and Get" Approaches to Professional Development

A solid and oft-cited report on the limitations of traditional professional development and recommendations for "learning systems" in schools is *Professional Learning in the Learning Profession: A Status Report on Teacher Development in the United States and Abroad* (2009) by Linda Darling-Hammond, Ruth Chung Wei, Alethea Andree, Nikole Richardson, and Stelios Orphanos.

Professional Learning Teams

In my book *Learnership: Invest in Teachers, Focus on Learning, and Put Test Scores in Perspective* (Toll, 2012), I wrote about professional learning teams and how they can be successful. Here are some points I made:

- Learning is optimized when teachers have a say in the topics and paths for learning.

- Learning teams struggle if there is not clarity in roles, processes for attending to differences among members, and engagement of all participants.

- Professional learning teams must have adequate time for their work.

Being Present in the Moment

There are many resources to help one learn to be more present in the moment. Two that may be of interest are *Mindfulness for Beginners: Reclaiming the Present Moment—And Your Life* by Jon Kabat-Zinn (2012) and *The Power of Now: A Guide to Spiritual Enlightenment* by Eckhart Tolle (2004).

Chapter 2

Changes Produced by Educational Coaching

An excellent overview of the research on coaching effectiveness can be found in the first chapter of *Coaching Matters* (Killion, Harrison, Bryan, & Clifton, 2012).

The authors provide a three-page list of studies that have found a positive effect of educational coaching, with outcomes ranging from greater implementation of initiatives to increased student achievement.

Leadership That Supports Coaching and Student Learning

I have written about *learnership,* my term to describe the leadership for learning provided by many effective principals and teacher leaders (Toll, 2012).

Flexible Implementation of Initiatives

Quite a few researchers have highlighted the value of implementing innovations flexibly to fit different contexts, as opposed to a one-size-fits-all fidelity-of-implementation model. See, for instance, McDonald, Keesler, Kauffman, and Schneider (2006) or an influential series of studies called the Change Agent Studies (RAND Corporation, 1977).

Characteristics of Teachers That Lead to Student Achievement

A report by the Center for Public Education (2005) synthesizes research on teacher qualities that impact student achievement. Not surprisingly, content knowledge, experience, and professional preparation matter. Another report, sponsored by the Comprehensive Center for Teacher Quality (Goe & Stickler, 2008), examines research on student achievement as it relates to teacher qualifications, characteristics, and practices. Interestingly, the report also indicates the limitations of observation tools for determining teacher effectiveness.

Avoiding Professional Development Focused on Teacher Behavior

Many researchers and educators have posited the importance of including reflection, understanding of content, and attention to teacher beliefs as essentials if practices are to change. Richardson and Placier (2001) provide a thorough review of research on professional development and on the lack of evidence that practice-only-focused professional development is effective. Gabriel Diaz-Maggioli (2004) points out the problematic nature of providing professional development focused only on technical aspects of what teachers do. Kathryn Egawa (2009) provides reflections on her personal journey as a teacher; the rich experiences she relates go far beyond just a focus on what she did.

Teacher Feelings and Student Achievement

Although teachers' positive feelings do not necessarily lead to greater student achievement, there certainly is evidence that teachers' stress or negative feelings can be harmful to students and negatively affect the school environment. Hinds, Jones, Gau, Forrester, and Biglan (2015) provide statistics on the prevalence of teacher stress and attempts to avoid noticing those feelings. Skaalvik and Skaalvik (2011) report on the increased likelihood of teachers leaving the profession when they're in unhappy work situations. For an overview of the role and influence of emotions in teaching, see Hargreaves (1998).

Teacher Thinking and Student Achievement

A great deal has been written about teacher reflection and understanding and their impact on student learning. Marzano, Pickering, Heflebower, Boogren, and Kanold-McIntyre (2012) provide a good overview and many suggestions for enhancing teacher reflection.

Next Generation Science Standards

You can find more information about the Next Generation Science Standards (NGSS) at www.nextgenscience.org/.

Principals Working with Teachers from a Coaching Stance

For several years, the National Staff Development Council, now called Learning Forward, published an online newsletter/blog called *The Learning Principal*. It still is valuable and includes several pieces about how principals can use a coaching stance in their own work. See https://learningforward.org/publications/learning-principal.

Teachers Directing the Change Process

A white paper from the organizations Learning Forward and the National Commission on Teaching and America's Future (Calvert, 2016) emphasizes the importance of teacher agency in professional development. In fact, the paper suggests that giving teachers control of their professional learning is a necessary component of effective learning and that it's missing from most professional development initiatives.

Chapter 4

The Coaching Problem-Solving Cycle

I provide greater detail about the problem-solving cycle, including why it's superior to the ways that teachers tend to solve problems and the ways that policymakers and administrators think problems are solved, in an article I wrote for *The Reading Teacher* (Toll, 2016).

Adult Learning

The best summary of the research on adult learning that I've found was developed by a team at Fermilab, a federal physics research lab (see Cave, LaMaster, & White, 1998).

People Don't Make Data-Driven Decisions

The economist Daniel Ariely (2009) provides evidence and explanation for the reality that humans are not very good at making data-driven decisions.

Chapter 5

Transitioning to a New Role

Chval, Arbaugh, Lannin, van Garderen, Cummings, Estapa, and Huey (2010) conducted a study of new math coaches that led them to conclude that coaches' successes and struggles in their first year are connected to the identities they have for themselves and the roles they ascribe to coaches.

Need for Professional Development for Coaches

Among those who recognize that there is not enough professional development for coaches are Blachowicz, Buhle, Ogle, Frost, Correa, and Kinner (2010); Gallucci, Van Lare, Yoon, and Boatright (2010); and Heineke (2013). I speculate that this professional development is lacking for two reasons: because of the assumption that as experienced, successful teachers, coaches don't need more help, and because coaches are usually small in number in schools and districts, so they may be overlooked when funding for professional development is limited.

Questioning One's Worth as a Coach

Coaches who feel unworthy to be a coach may want to investigate the concept of *the imposter syndrome,* which is the idea that one is not qualified or skilled enough to be in the position one has, despite external evidence of one's competence. There are many online resources for learning about this concept.

Chapter 6
Manipulative Language

Claire Newton provides an overview of what manipulative language sounds and feels like, along with an overview of other styles of communication: assertive, aggressive, passive-aggressive, and submissive. See www.clairenewton. co.za/my-articles/the-five-communication-styles.html.

People Are Always Changing

Those who study complex living systems point out that anything that is alive is changing because growth is inherent to being alive. This idea contradicts assumptions among some educators that there are teachers who have stopped growing or learning. Sometimes we fail to see where the change is occurring. Davis and Sumara (2006) explain this idea further. Richardson and Placier (2001) highlight approaches to professional development that acknowledge teachers' ongoing learning, which they call *naturalistic professional development.*

Chapter 7
PLTs and PLCs

The concept of the professional learning community was created to describe a workplace in which learning was given a priority. It didn't refer specifically to small teams of employees. (See Senge, 2006, for instance.) However, in many such workplaces, people did break into teams and learn collaboratively within those teams; thus, *professional learning community* became a term that was applied to teams as well as entire workplaces. To avoid confusion, though, I use the term *professional learning team,* or PLT, when referring to small teams in schools.

Rewards for Students Reading a Certain Amount Each Evening

Alfie Kohn (1999) presents the definitive set of arguments against "carrot and stick" systems for directing children's (and adults') behavior. I once wrote an essay for *Reading Today* about why I, as a school principal, didn't sit on the school roof as a reward for students' reading—or encourage other rewards that had nothing to do with the benefits of reading itself (Toll, 1996).

Chapter 8

Anxiety

Parker Palmer (2007) reflects on fear as the biggest limitation on his teaching successes, and it seems to me that fear is a kind of anxiety.

Resistance

Although I generally avoid the term *resistance* when speaking about teachers who would rather not work with a coach, because the term is used pejoratively, I did learn a great deal about anxiety that manifests itself as resistance when I read a book from the field of psychology titled *Working with Resistance* (Stark, 2002).

Mirror Neurons

Scientific American (n.d.) ran an interesting article about mirror neurons, featuring an interview with neuroscientist Marco Iacoboni, at www.scientific american.com/article/the-mirror-neuron-revolut/.

The Problem with Triangulation

Marc Hannum (2015) provides a leadership-focused view of the problems with triangulation in communication in organizations. See http://blog.linkageinc. com/blog/systems-thinking-5-the-toxic-effects-of-communication-triangulation/.

Time Shortage

Many authors have noted the need for coaches to have more time to do their work, including Poglinco, Bach, Hovde, Rosenblum, Saunders, and Supovitz (2003); Smith (2006); Marsh and colleagues (2008); and Lynch and Ferguson (2010).

Chapter 9
Research on Adult Learning

Again, see Cave, LaMaster, and White, 1998, a great resource on the characteristics of adult learners.

Book Discussion Groups

Burbank, Kauchak, and Bates (2010) compared the experiences of preservice teachers and inservice teachers when they participated in book groups. They found that inexperienced teachers used the book groups to develop understandings and practices. More experienced teachers, while sometimes enhancing their knowledge and skills, also benefited by engaging in reader response in a personally enriching way. Both groups of teachers saw the need for book groups to be facilitated. The American Library Association provides many resources for book discussion groups at http://libguides.ala.org/book discussiongroups.

Emergent Bilingual Students

Some educators are using the term *emergent bilingual* as a better way to describe students who first learned a language other than English and who now are learning English because it conveys that the students are learning to be bilingual rather than solely learning English (see Escamilla & Hopewell, 2010).

Concerns About Whole-Group Professional Development

See the bibliographic entry for Chapter 1 related to "sit and get" professional development.

Chapter 10

Coaches Need More Professional Development

See the bibliographic entry for Chapter 5 for resources on the need for coaches to have more professional development.

Change

Hall and Hord (2001) provide a thorough consideration of change in schools.

Complex Living Systems

The research on complex living systems provides a fascinating insight into how schools, classrooms, faculties, and other systems function and how change occurs. I find the work of Brent Davis and Dennis Sumara (2006) most helpful in this area because they write as educators themselves.

Listening Carefully as a Way to Appreciate Teachers

Roger Fisher and Daniel Shapiro (2006) posit that when conversations turn difficult, it's because one or more participants fail to have their human concerns attended to. Of the five human concerns they highlight, one—appreciation—is often experienced by being listened to closely.

Need for Professional Development for Coaches

See the bibliographic entry for Chapter 5.

Index

Note: The letter *f* following a page number denotes a figure.

About the Author

 **Cathy A. Toll** supports teacher learning by guiding educational coaches, professional learning teams, and administrative leaders. She has been a consultant, keynote speaker, and workshop leader throughout the United States, Australia, and Canada. Toll has served as a teacher at the elementary, middle, and high school levels, reading specialist, curriculum coordinator, school principal, director of literacy research and development, grant director, state department of education consultant, and educational coach. She has published widely for teacher leaders, including six books for literacy coaches and a book on learnership for principals and teacher leaders. Toll is chair of the Department of Literacy and Language at the University of Wisconsin Oshkosh. She can be reached at cathy@partneringtolearn.com. Her website is www.partneringtolearn.com.

Related ASCD Resources

At the time of publication, the following resources were available (ASCD stock numbers in parentheses).

Print Products

The Coach Approach to School Leadership: Leading Teachers to Higher Levels of Effectiveness by Jessica Johnson, Shira Leibowitz, and Kathy Perret (#117025)

Creating a Culture of Reflective Practice: Capacity-Building for Schoolwide Success by Pete Hall and Alisa Simeral (#117006)

Instructional Coaching in Action: An Integrated Approach That Transforms Thinking, Practice, and Schools by Ellen B. Eisenberg, Bruce P. Eisenberg, Elliott A. Medrich, and Ivan Charner (#117028)

Peer Coaching to Enrich Professional Practice, School Culture, and Student Learning by Pam Robbins (#115014)

For up-to-date information about ASCD resources, go to **www.ascd.org**. You can search the complete archives of *Educational Leadership* at **www.ascd.org/el.**

ASCD myTeachSource®

Download resources from a professional learning platform with hundreds of research-based best practices and tools for your classroom at http://myteach source.ascd.org/

For more information, send an e-mail to member@ascd.org; call 1-800-933-2723 or 703-578-9600; send a fax to 703-575-5400; or write to Information Services, ASCD, 1703 N. Beauregard St., Alexandria, VA 22311-1714 USA.